DO YOU KNOW
HILCHOS
YOM TOV?

Compiled by
Rabbi Michoel Fletcher

MENUCHA PUBLISHERS

אפרים נחום ב"ר אברהם ז"ל

נפטר לעולמו י' אלול תשע"ח

Mr Ephraim Pinnick ז"ל

An outstanding member of
the Gateshead Kehilla
and of Anglo Jewry.

He established and ran the Gateshead Yarchei Kalloh
for many decades attracting Yidden from different
backgrounds to spend a holiday with their family in a Torah
atmosphere.

The men learned all morning and there were shiurim in the
evening for men and women with activities for children.

We all left physically refreshed and spiritually inspired.

He was a Ba'al Tzedoko and Ba'al Chessed with great yiras
Shomayim and kovod Talmidei Chachomim.

"כל המזכה את הרבים זכות הרבים תלוי בו"

פרקי אבות ה' כ"א

Rabbi **Hillel A. Asher**

22/4 Nadvorna st.
Beitar Ellit, Israel
052-7610424

הלל אהרן אשר

רח' הרבי מנדבורנא 22/4
ביתר עילית
052-7610424

ב"ה

יום כ"ז מרחשון ה'תשע"ט

הסכמה וברכה

שמחתי שמחה גדולה לראות את הספר החשוב על הלכות יום-טוב, הכתוב בשפת האנגלית, ונקרא שמו "?Do You Know Hilchos Yom Tov". הספר נכתב על ידי הרב **מיכאל פלעטשר** שליט"א שכבר מוכר זה זמן רב בשערים המצויים בהלכה, ע"י ספריו הקודמים על הלכות שבת, ברכות, חול המועד ועוד.

כבוד הרב המחבר ביקש ממני לעבור על תוכן ספרו הנוכחי, בגדר טובים השנים מן האחד. ולמרות שלדעתי אין הוא צריך כלל להסכמתי, רצונו אעשה ואני מעיד שעברתי על כל סעיף וסעיף המובא בספר - עד כמה שידי הכהה מגעת, והערתי בכמה מקומות כפי שחנני ה', ופלפלתי יחד בכמה וכמה הלכות, עד שיצא דבר ברור ומתוקן אליבא דהלכתא.

בהרבה הלכות ישנם דעות שונות בדברי הפוסקים, והמחבר הנכבד עמל הרבה כדי להביא את ההלכה למעשה לדעת רוב הפוסקים האחרונים, ובמקומות שיש דעה אחרת המקובלת, השתדל לציין זאת בגוף הספר. כבוד רב הוא לי לכתוב מכתב הסכמה וברכה לספר, שלענ"ד כל התוכן ראוי לסמוך עליו הלכה למעשה.

הספר הזה יחיד במינו, ונכתב באופן מתאים ומיוחד לדורנו, באופן של שאלות ותשובות - בסדר ברור ובצורה מושכת, כביכול מתנהל שיחה בין התלמיד לרב. השאלות כולן הינן מאד נוגעות למעשה בבית היהודי המודרני, עד שהמתחיל ללמוד את התוכן לא ירצה להניחו מידיו. אמנם למרות סגנונו הקל של הספר, ההלכות עצמן הינן פירות של עמל ויגיעה של המחבר שליט"א, שהשקיע כוחותיו גדולים, עד שיצא הלכה למעשה.

ברכתי שהרב שליט"א ימשיך לזכות לסייעתא דשמיא, שמעיינותיו יפוצו חוצה, ובתפילה ובתחינה שלא תצא מכשול מתחת ידו, ויזכה בספרא זה ובכל ספריו ובכל פעולותיו הברוכים, לזכות את הרבים ולהרביץ תורה בישראל, עד ביאת הגואל בב"א.

הכותב לכבוד התורה,

הלל אהרן אשר

Rabbi **Hillel A. Asher**

22/4 Nadvorna st.
Beitar Ellit, Israel
052-7610424

חלל אהרן אשר

רח׳ הרבי מנדבורנא 22/4
ביתר עילית
052–7610424

יוֹם א׳ טֵבֵת ה'תִשׁעֵ"ט

ב"ה

I feel privileged to have seen this valuable *sefer* Do You Know Hilchos Yom Tov? It is written by Rabbi Michoel Fletcher שליט"א who is already well-known for his previous excellent *sefarim* on *halacha* and *hashkafa*.

He has asked me to check the text of this *sefer* to confirm that everything is correct although, in my view, someone of his stature and proficiency has no need of my agreement. Having gone through the entire text carefully, I fully agree with all his conclusions. In my humble opinion, everything in this wonderful *sefer* can be relied on *halacha l'maase*. Where there is a halachic dispute, the author has correctly ascertained the majority view that we should follow.

The *sefer* itself is unique, written in a way that is most appropriate for our generation. The situations mentioned are precisely those that confront every observant Jewish family on Yom Tov. The text is in the form of a conversation between a *rav* and *talmid* and is light and compelling. Through the informal style, the author brings warmth to the subject of *hilchos Yom Tov*. The reader is genuinely infused with the *simcha* which is in itself a central *mitzva* of *Yom Tov*.

My *brocha* is that Rabbi Fletcher שליט"א should continue to teach Torah to our generation in his inimitable style, which increases both the care with which we observe the *mitzvos* and our love for Torah itself. He should enjoy good health to write new *sefarim* on different subjects from which we can all learn from and be inspired by for many years to come.

Rav Hillel Asher
Rav and Posek in Beitar, Eretz Yisroel

HASKAMOS TO THE AUTHOR'S PREVIOUS SEFARIM
RECEIVED FROM
(in alphabetical order):

Rav Moshe Heinemann, א"טילש
Rav and *Av Beis Din*, Baltimore, MD

Rav Elimelech Kornfeld, א"טילש
Rav, Kehillas HaGra, Ramat Beit Shemesh, MD

Dayan Gavriel Krausz, א"טילש
Rosh Beis Din, Manchester, England

Rav Zev Leff, א"טילש
Rav and *Rosh Yeshivah*, Moshav Mattisyahu

Rav Shlomo Zalman Perlstein, א"טילש
Mara D'Asra, Ramat Beit Shemesh Alef

Rav Mattisyahu Salomon, א"טילש
Mashgiach Ruchani, Beth Medrash Govoha, Lakewood, NJ

Rav Moshe Sternbuch, א"טילש
Rosh Beis Din, Eidah Chareidis, Yerushalayim

Rav Avrohom Weiss, א"טילש
Former *Av Beis Din*, Glasgow, Scotland

Rav Tuvya Weiss, א"טילש
Av Beis Din, Eidah Chareidis, Yerushalayim

Rav Shraga Feivel Zimmerman, א"טילש
Mara D'Asra, Gateshead, England

Preface

*D*o You Know Hilchos Yom Tov? complements *Do You Know Hilchos Chol Hamoed?* in covering what every Jewish home needs to know over Yom Tov. They both complement *Do You Know Hilchos Shabbos?* which details what we all need to know on Shabbos. The *halachos* are similar but there are important differences as well, which can easily lead to confusion.

Learning *halachos* can seem to be too demanding for all but the most studious. That is why I have written these *sefarim* in a lighter style, as a conversation between a willing student and teacher covering actual situations which we all face on Shabbos, Yom Tov and Chol Hamoed. Many families enjoy learning these *sefarim* as they sit round their Shabbos and Yom Tov tables, with everyone taking a turn to ask the others a question. For those who need to look up a particular *halacha,* there is a detailed index.

I must particularly thank Rav Hillel Asher *shlita* of Beitar, who is acknowledged as an expert *posek* in all areas of *halacha.* He scrutinized the text checking that my conclusions are all correct. After a few discussions and some changes he was able to say that he agreed with everything I had written.

A *sefer* on *halacha* either brings different opinions and tells the reader to consult their rav, or says clearly what the correct *halacha* is, at least according to most *Poskim.* My *sefarim* follow the second style because I think most readers want to learn a *sefer* to find out what they should do. Many people, unfortunately, do not have a rav whom they can easily consult, and for them, a *sefer* on *halacha* without conclusions is frustrating and of limited use. Of course, if a writer does write conclusions, a big responsibility lies on him to be accurate. The help of an acknowledged expert is vital to being certain that the conclusions are correct. So thank you again, Rav Asher.

Mrs. Tova Younger edited this sefer, Mrs. Deena Weinberg did the typesetting and Mrs. Jocy Sades designed the cover. The indexer and proofreader did not want to be mentioned by name but I include them in my sincere thanks to each who helped polish this sefer with their attention to detail and accuracy. My wife also prefers not to be mentioned, but, needless to say, without her, I could not have written any *sefarim*.

My constant thanks go to Hashem for giving me the *zechus* to learn and teach Torah and my *tefilla* is that I merit to receive *siyata d'Shmaya* to continue my *avodas hakodesh* for many more years, together with my wife, family and all the readers of my *sefarim*.

Michoel Fletcher
Ramat Beit Shemesh, Teves 5779

Contents

QUIZ

What is the relevance of the pictures on the front cover to Hilchos Yom Tov?

1. Sefer Torah
2. Plate of delicious food
3. Stroller
4. Pot cooking
5. Grater
6. Sukkah
7. Piece of chicken and matzah
8. Flag
9. Oranges

Answers

1. Chapter 6, answer 1 and the Yom Tov of Shavuos.
2. Chapter 2, answer 5.
3. Chapter 9, answer 14.
4. Chapter 5, answers 1 and 2.
5. Chapter 11, answers 10 and 11.
6. Chapter 12, answer 14 and the Yom Tov of Sukkos
7. Chapter 15, answers 7 and 8 and the Yom Tov of Pesach.
8. Chapter 9, answer 9 and the Yom Tov of Simchas Torah.
9. Chapter 13, question 10.

Chapter One
The Purpose of *Yom Tov*

1. *Before I ask you **what** the halachos of Yom Tov are, please tell me **why** the Torah tells us to keep the Yomim Tovim.*

    Each Yom Tov has its own reason. Pesach commemorates Hashem's bringing us out of Mitzrayim in a miraculous way. Shavuos celebrates the giving of the Torah to the Jewish people and Sukkos reminds us of how Hashem protected us in the wilderness after He brought us out of Mitzrayim.[1] Shemini Atzeres follows immediately after Sukkos and is traditionally understood as an extra opportunity to rejoice with Hashem at the end of our *zman simchaseinu*.

2. *If so, why is Sukkos in the fall? Shouldn't it be in the spring when we first left Mitzrayim and entered the wilderness?*

    The best-known answer to this question is given by the *Tur* (O.C. 625). He says Sukkos requires us to live in a *sukkah* for a whole week, which wouldn't be noticeable in the spring because the weather is getting warmer and people tend to go outside anyway. Therefore the Torah says that we should

---

1. According to one opinion we remember particularly the physical Sukkos in which we lived in the wilderness (*Sukkos Mamash*). According to another opinion we focus on the *Ananei Hakavod* – the Clouds of Glory which surrounded the whole camp. See *Sukkos* 11a.

keep Sukkos in the fall when it is getting colder and people are spending more time inside their homes. This way when we go outside into our sukkah it is clear that we are doing this for the purpose of the *mitzvah*.

3. *Isn't one of the central features of the Yomim Tovim that we have to leave our homes to be oleh regel to the Beis Hamikdash in Yerushalayim? Since we have no Beis Hamikdash at the moment, is there any point in keeping the other mitzvos of Yom Tov?*

You may have heard the story of the woman who was selling apples in the market when some unruly boys upset her barrel full of apples and as they rolled around, stole as much as they could. Very aggravated, she ran to the police to complain. They told her that they would try to find the culprits but in the meantime she should hurry back to the market to grab the remaining apples. They told her, "Just because you have lost some of your apples, it doesn't mean you have to lose all of them." So although it is true we cannot perform the mitzvah of *aliyah l'regel*, that doesn't mean that we shouldn't do those mitzvos of Yom Tov which we can do. Incidentally there is a custom to visit the Kosel on Yom Tov or to go to the nearest point that we can reach.[2]

4. *When should I start learning the halachos of Yom Tov?*

Thirty days before Yom Tov. Some say that this is only before Pesach because of the many *halachos* involved but concerning the other Yomim Tovim a few days is enough.[3]

---

2 Brought by the Ran on *Taanis* 10a
3. See Mishna Berura 429:1

5. *I heard that even though we should always be b'simchah, especially on Shabbos,*[4] *on Yom Tov it is even more important. Is this true and why?*

Yes, on Yom Tov there is a specific mitzvah to be *b'simchah*. The daily *simchah* which we should always feel is because of our *emunah* that Hashem has created the world and that we are privileged to serve Him; this is our focus particularly on Shabbos. In addition to this, on Yom Tov we remember specific kindnesses which He did for us at this time of the year such as bringing us out of Mitzrayim, looking after us in the wilderness, and giving us the Torah as we mentioned above.

6. *Maybe we should start learning hilchos Yom Tov with the halachos of simchas Yom Tov.*

An excellent idea.

---

4. All sefarim talk about the importance of being b'simchah especially when we are doing mitzvos and especially as we keep the very important mitzva of Shabbos.

Chapter Two
Hilchos Simchas Yom Tov

1. *Before we go into the halachos of the mitzvah of simchah, can you give me guidance on how I can develop a feeling of simchah?*

    The wording of the *Yom Tov Shemoneh Esrei* gives us clear guidance on how to build *simchah* inside us. "*Atoh vechartonu mikol ho'amim...*You have chosen us from all peoples, You have loved us, You have desired us, You have elevated us above all nations, You have sanctified us with Your *mitzvos*, You have drawn us near to Your service, and You have proclaimed Your great and holy Name upon us." If we contemplate these words throughout Yom Tov they will infuse us with appreciation to Hashem for giving us this treasured status. This will be our springboard for deep *simchas Yom Tov*.[5]

2. *Do we all have this mitzvah of rejoicing on Yom Tov?*

    Yes; men, women and children.[6]

---

5. The Rambam *Hilchos Yom Tov* 6:17 writes that we have to be *same'ach v'tov lev*. The *Chut Shoni Hilchos Yom Tov Perek* 22 explains that when the Rambam says "*vetov* lev" he is telling us that besides eating and drinking which gives us *simchah*, there is another part of the mitzvah; that is to feel *simchah* in one's heart. My family and I have the *minhag* to sing *Atah Vechartanu* during our daytime *seudah*, and after each phrase we think of how privileged we are and enjoy a SMALL *l'chaim*; I highly recommend it.
6. Shulchan Aruch 529;2 See *Chut Shoni* (ibid) that the *halachah* of a child being

3. *But Shloimele, who's only one, is surely too young to have to keep mitzvos.*

Yes, I am talking about children who are old enough to understand about Yom Tov. But it's never too early to start. Tell him that he will have ice-cream today because it's Yom Tov and he'll get the idea that Yom Tov is sweet.

4. *So besides thinking about the ideas you mentioned earlier, we have to promote simchah in practical ways?*

Yes. Our *tefillos* should bring us *simchah*, especially Hallel which we say on every Yom Tov. And men should spend time learning Torah which also should be a source of *simchah*. In fact, the total amount of time spent on *davening* and learning should be half the day.

5. *What about eating good food?*

We also have to eat two festive *seudos*, each beginning with *lechem mishnah*, one by night and one by day.[7] There is a mitzvah to eat a particularly tasty meal on Shavuos to "show how happy we are that we received the Torah."[8] Even though there is no obligation of *seudah shelishis* on Yom Tov, some *Poskim* recommend eating fruit or at least an extra dish during the morning *seudah* as a symbolic substitute for *seudah shelishis*. Other details are subjective. A man's *simchah* will be enhanced by eating meat

---

b'simchah is not the child's mitzvah if he is below the age of *chinuch* but rather it is the father's mitzvah to ensure that all his family should be *b'simchah*. Nevertheless, the child has to have a concept that it is Yom Tov as distinct from a weekday, before this mitzvah applies to him.

7. There is an opinion that women are not obliged to have a *seudah* on Yom Tov. Although the *halachah* is that they are obliged, if they forgot *ya'ale v'yavo* in *Birkas Hamazon* they do not repeat the *benching*.

8. *Pesachim* 68b and see Rashi's commentary.

and drinking wine. He should also wear his nicest clothes, even better than his Shabbos clothes.[9] Women also enjoy good meals and good clothes, of course, but they particularly like to wear *new* clothes or jewelry so a husband should buy his wife something new for Yom Tov according to his means.[10] Children like candies and therefore should be given Yom Tov treats. Of course, children value their parents' attention and even though Yom Tov is often a busy time, parents should not be too busy to give their children quality time.

6. *Avi loves stories—should I prepare some good ones to tell him?*

Children love stories and preparing age-appropriate stories for them should definitely be part of their parents' *Shabbos* and *Yom Tov* preparations.

7. *Our teenage daughter has gone vegetarian. Should I tell her that she has to eat meat on Yom Tov?*

A person who doesn't like meat for any reason is not obliged to eat meat.[11]

8. *To be quite honest I'm a bit short of cash at the moment. Should we cut back on the frills and eat the minimum?*

One person's 'frills' are another person's 'basics.' How people spend their money also varies. If you are short of cash because you just bought the latest model car, it would be inappropriate to cut down on having plentiful food and new clothes for Yom Tov. Saving up for next season's "Unique *kosher l'mehadrin*

---

9. *Shulchan Aruch* 529:1
10. *Ibid.* 529:2
11. *Ibid.* 242:2

trip down the Amazon" is also no excuse. A person should be generous in spending on *Yom Tov*, in keeping with his regular life style.

To quote the *Poskim,*[12] "We should not cut down on *Yom Tov* expenses." And the *Mishnah Berurah*[13] quotes the Gemara[14] reminding us that, "A person's income is fixed every year on *Rosh Hashanah*, except for *Yom Tov* and *Shabbos* expenses about which one who spends less has his annual allocation reduced and one who spends more has his annual allocation increased."[15]

9. Am I obliged to borrow money to pay for simchas Yom Tov?

If you see how you will be able to pay back the loan, you should borrow money, if necessary, to fulfill *simchas Yom Tov.* If you do not have a practical way to repay the loan, there is a dispute amongst the *Poskim.*[16] The conclusion is that one should certainly not borrow more money than needed for basic requirements.[17]

10. We always have guests for Yom Tov meals. Tatty says that it is a big mitzvah.

Your *Tatty* is right, especially regarding those people who would otherwise be on their own. My only comment is that

---

12. *Shulchan Aruch* O.C. 529:1
13. *Ibid.* 2
14. *Beitzah* 16a
15. The *Biur Halachah* comments on this: "If a person spends money on unnecessary luxuries, his total allocation will not be increased, leaving him with a possible shortfall. This, in turn, can lead to attempts to earn illegal money, which, besides being forbidden, could bring a person to a place which he certainly wouldn't want to be in."
16. *Shaarei Tziyun* 242:12. He concludes that there is no general rule.
17. See the subject discussed at length in *Chut Shoni Hilchos Shabbos Perek One Halachah Two.*

people don't like to feel that they are somebody's "mitzvah". Welcome them warmly, telling them that *Yom Tov* wouldn't be the same without them. Make them feel–and indeed *you* should feel–that *they* are doing *you* the favor by accepting your invitation.[18]

11. *It seems like a great mitzvah to eat the best foods and drink the best wine. What's the snag?*

There's no snag, but you have to remember not to eat or drink too much. *Yom Tov* is not supposed to be a time to overeat or even to eat just because you like the food. It is an opportunity to serve Hashem through *simchah*, which is a high level of *Avodas Hashem*. Our classic commentators[19] say that chassidim who know Hashem and continually feel His presence, praise Hashem at a time of *simchah* more and more for giving them this *simchah*.

12. *I presume that all the halachos of Shabbos about not doing or reading things which make a person sad apply on Yom Tov as well.*

It is even more important on *Yom Tov* because of the mitzvah to be *b'simchah*.

13. *Does the mitzvah of simchah apply on Rosh Hashanah?*

Yes.[20]

---

18. My good friend and colleague Rav Yehonoson Gefen once brought an explanation *al derech drush* of the statement of *Chazal* that a person who gives *tzedakah* "on the condition that my son lives," is a complete tzaddik. This is when the donor, in order to save the poor recipient's embarrassment, explains to him that his accepting this *tzedakah* will do the donor a big favor, because in the merit of this *tzedakah*, his son will recover.

19. *Tur* (ibid) and *Mishnah Berurah* 529:21

20. *Mishnah Berurah* 597:1

14. *How can we be happy on Rosh Hashanah when we're being judged? Aren't Rosh Hashanah and Yom Kippur called the Yamim Nora'im – the Days of Awe?*

It is true that because of the seriousness of the day external signs of *simchah* should be somewhat limited; we do not wear our most elegant clothes[21] and we do not eat as expansively as we might have done.[22] However we should still be *b'simchah*. Firstly, "We have trust in the kindness of Hashem that He will judge us favorably."[23] Also we are happy to be among those who are crowning Hashem as the King of the Universe and living according to His commandments rather than being among those who waste their lives in pursuing honor, riches and physical pleasures and never achieve true contentment.

---

21. *Ibid.* 582:25
22. *Shulchan Aruch* 597:1
23. *Mishnah Berurah* 582:25

Chapter Three
Differences between *Halachos* of Shabbos and *Yom Tov*

1. *Why are the halachos of Yom Tov different than the halachos of Shabbos?*

   A possible explanation is that since the Torah wants us to be particularly happy on Yom Tov, we are allowed to do those *melachos* which would otherwise have prevented us from eating freshly prepared foods, which are usually tastier than foods prepared in advance. This will increase our *simchah*. This explanation is supported by the Ashkenazi custom in *Chutz La'aretz regarding duchening (Birkas Kohanim)*. The *kohanim* do not *duchan* during the year because they are lacking in *simchah*. On Yom Tov they do, but only at *Mussaf*, shortly before they will eat their *Yom Tov seudah*.[24] Only then, apparently, is a person in a state of peak happiness. We see that *simchah* and eating are inextricably mixed.[25]

2. *Does that mean that anything which contributes to food preparation is permitted?*

---

24. See *Rama* 128:44
25. For an explanation more *al derech nistar* see *Derech Hashem* 4:7

No. There are many details about what is permitted and what is not. It is precisely to clarify these issues that I am *b'ezras Hashem* writing this *sefer*.

3. *Where does the Torah tell us that food preparation is permitted on Yom Tov, subject, of course, to the details which I am looking forward to learning?*

In *Parshas Bo*[26] the Torah says, "The first day and the seventh day of Pesach will be holy and no *melachos* shall be done on them; but for what is necessary for you to eat, those *melachos* may be done." Without going into the finer points about how we know that this applies to all Yomim Tovim[27], this is our clearest source that there are certain differences between the *halachos* of Yom Tov and the *halachos* of Shabbos.

4. *Why can't we just take this at face value and allow all food preparation?*

There are many sources in the words of *Chazal* that indicate that not all food preparation is permitted. *Beitzah* 3a indicates that picking fruit from a tree to eat is not allowed on Yom Tov. Later the mishnah (23b) doesn't allow catching fish from a pond even to eat it on Yom Tov. *Kesuvos* 7a says that we may do a *melachah* even for food only if it is *shaveh l'kol nefesh* – suitable for an average person. And the *Mishnah* in *Beitzah* 12a allows carrying a *sefer Torah* in the street or a child for its *bris* even though these are not for food. We see that there is much more to *Hilchos Yom Tov* than what a cursory reading of the *pasuk* suggests.

---

26. *Shemos* 12:16
27. Including *Rosh Hashanah* which is discussed in the early commentators.

5. *How do the commentators understand these prohibitions of picking fruit from a tree and trapping fish? I think it would increase my simchas Yom Tov to be allowed to eat a freshly picked apple or freshly caught fish, especially if I couldn't get any before Yom Tov.*

The *Rishonim* give different explanations. Some say that only those *melachos* from the *melachah* of kneading in the list of the 39 *melachos* are permitted. Other *melachos* are not allowed according to the Torah, even though they are part of the preparation of food. Others say that according to the Torah, *melachos* like *kotzer* (harvesting fruit and vegetables from the place where they grew) and *tzad* (trapping animals, birds or fish) are permitted but *Chazal* forbade them because they are usually done in much larger quantities than a person needs for one day. The full list of *melachos* involved in food preparation which are forbidden according to this opinion are reaping, grinding, threshing (which includes squeezing juice from fruit), sieving and trapping.[28] Chazal, in their wisdom, wanted to reduce the risk of our spending Yom Tov doing these 'permitted' *halachos*, instead of celebrating Yom Tov as we should. Doing a *melachah* for after Yom Tov is not allowed, so they forbade those *melachos* completely. We should be grateful to *Chazal* for fulfilling their responsibilities to protect the Torah. Without their rabbinic laws we could spend the whole of Shabbos and Yom Tov doing activities which are technically not forbidden by the Torah, but would ruin the whole spirit of the day.

6. *Are we never allowed to prepare on Yom Tov for after Yom Tov? What happens when Yom Tov falls on Erev Shabbos?*

Good point. You are correct; we are not allowed to prepare on Yom Tov for after Yom Tov except for the instance you give,

---

28. *Shulchan Aruch* 495:2 and *Mishnah Berurah* 495:13

when Yom Tov falls on Erev Shabbos. And we can do these preparations only if we make an *eiruv tavshilin*. We will learn the *halachos* about the *eiruv tavshilin* in a later chapter.[29]

7.   *Do I have to make sure that I don't cook more than we strictly need on Yom Tov to ensure I will not have cooked food on Yom Tov for after Yom Tov?*

You may cook as much as you may need even if it probably won't be eaten.

8.   *I have a friend who sometimes drops in unexpectedly on Yom Tov afternoon. May I also take her into account even though she may not come?*

If there is a reasonable chance that she might come, you can cook extra in case.[30]

9.   *Does this apply even if the day after Yom Tov is Chol Hamoed?*
Yes.[31]

10.   *Is the halachah also the same if the next day is Yom Tov Sheini?*
Yes.[32]

29. Chapter 15.
30. *Yom Tov Kehilchasah* 6:2. If there is only a small chance that the guest might come, one should cook more of the same food in the same pan, a leniency which IYH we will describe in detail in Chapter Five.
31. *Shulchan Aruch* 503:1 forbids cooking even for *Yom Tov Sheini*.
32. *Ibid.*

Chapter Four
Yom Tov Sheini

1. *Why is there a second day of Yom Tov?*

The Beis Din in Jerusalem used to consecrate each new Jewish month when they heard the testimony of two witnesses who had seen the New Moon. The Beis Din would then dispatch messengers to tell all the Jewish communities when the new month began, so that they would know when to celebrate the festivals. The crucial issue was whether the previous month had lasted twenty-nine or thirty days. Since messengers were unlikely to reach communities outside the Land of Israel before the festival was to occur, these communities kept the festivals for two days rather than one, in order to be certain that they were celebrating the right day. Even though we no longer rely on witnesses to begin a new month and there should be no confusion, *Chazal* were concerned that wars or other chaotic conditions might prevent people from knowing the exact date of the festivals. They therefore enacted that all communities outside of Eretz Yisroel[33] should continue keeping two days of Yom Tov.[34]

---

33. The consensus opinion of the *Poskim* is that Eilat which is part of the State of Israel, though it is *halachically* regarded as *Chutz La'aretz* for other *halachos*, keeps one day of Yom Tov (*Teshuvos Vehanhogos* 3:332).
34. *Beitzah* 5b and Rashi

2. *Is there a difference between the halachos of Yom Tov Rishon and Yom Tov Sheini?*

There are only two areas of difference. One is that we may treat a minor illness with medication or by transgressing a rabbinic prohibition on *Yom Tov Sheini*[35] whereas on *Yom Tov Rishon* this is only allowed if he needs to be in bed because of his illness. Secondly, there is a difference in the *halachos* of burying a deceased person. On *Yom Tov Rishon* we have to ask a non-Jew to dig a grave, but on *Yom Tov Sheini* even a Jew may dig the grave if there is no non-Jew readily available.[36] We will discuss these *halachos* in more detail in a later chapter. Besides these exceptions, the two days of Yom Tov have identical *halachos*. For the two days of Rosh Hashanah which are kept even in Eretz Yisroel, there are no differences between the first day and the second day.[37]

3. *We often visit Eretz Yisroel for Yom Tov and we have family there who sometimes comes to us for Yom Tov. This is where it begins to be complicated, isn't it?*

The accepted *halachah* is that even if you are in Eretz Yisroel where all the residents are keeping one day Yom Tov, you should keep two days.[38] The rule is that a person who is visiting another community but intends to return home has

---

35. *Shulchan Aruch* and *Rama* O.C. 496:2. The *Shaar Hatziun* (9) is unsure whether one may transgress a Torah prohibition done in an unusual way on *Yom Tov Sheini* for a person who has only a minor illness.
36. This is the Ashkenazi custom to ask a non-Jew even on the second day if he is readily available. The Sefardi custom is to allow a Jew to do the necessary *melachos* even if a non-Jew is available.
37. *Shulchan Aruch* 496:2 except for burying the dead as we shall see later
38. There is another opinion of the *Shulchan Aruch HaRav*, usually followed in Chabad communities, only to keep one day when visiting Eretz Yisroel. One may follow this ruling only if one follows the opinion of the *Shulchan Aruch HaRav* in all *halachos*.

to keep the stricter customs of the place he is coming from.[39]

4. *And when they are visiting us?*

Residents of Eretz Yisroel who are visiting Chutz La'aretz for Yom Tov are not allowed to do any *melachos* in your house, even in private, even though technically it will not be Yom Tov for them on the second day.[40]

5. *If it's not really Yom Tov for them, shouldn't they be wearing tefillin and davening the weekday Shemoneh Esrei?*

Yes, but it should be done in a way that other people don't notice, so they must wear *tefillin* in private. Why? If the local residents realize that some Jews are not keeping the second day of Yom Tov, it might lower their respect for the second day of Yom Tov. For the same reason, they have to do all the same mitzvos as the locals, such as lighting Yom Tov candles and all the mitzvos of *Seder* night although they do not say the relevant *brochos*. Even if there are ten or more *bnei Eretz Yisroel* in a community in Chutz La'aretz, they are not allowed to arrange a separate *davening*. The technical term for all this is *zilzelusa d'Yom Tov Sheini* (disrespect for *Yom Tov Sheini*) which the *halachah* is very particular to avoid.

6. *If they spend part of their holiday outside the Jewish community, do they have to keep Yom Tov Sheini there?*

If no Jews live there, no.

7. *What happens if there are only some non-religious Jews living in that place and no organized community?*

---

39. *Pesachim* 50a
40. *Mishnah Berurah* 496:9

One may not be lenient[41] because if a Jew, even a non-religious Jew, sees religious-looking Jews not keeping the second day Yom Tov, he might come to the conclusion that keeping a second day is not really necessary. One can never know -- he might have previously observed Yom Tov in some way and this will cause him to stop keeping it at all. He might later become religious but will still be of the opinion that the second day must be some kind of *chumrah*, which is not necessary to observe.

8.   *What happens if religious Jews from Eretz Yisroel and Chutz La'aretz are together at a holiday hotel where there is no permanent Jewish community?*

The *Poskim* distinguish between a hotel which is open for the whole year, where *bnei Eretz Yisroel* may not do *melachos* and a hotel which is just open for the week of Yom Tov where they may do *melachos*.[42]

9.   *I understand that another complicated area in these halachos is when people have moved from their original homes and are living in Eretz Yisroel or Chutz La'aretz for an extended period of time and they don't know for sure about their future.*

Probably more questions about *Yom Tov Sheini* are asked on this topic than any other. We have to appreciate that with today's ease of travel together with the 'global village' in which we live, answers to these questions will not always be the same as they were a hundred years ago. We move around with relative ease, follow career opportunities, move somewhere and then move back or elsewhere. Some people live half a year

41. *Igros Moshe* Y.D 4:24.2
42. *Yom Tov Sheini Kehilchasa* 3:13

in Eretz Yisroel and half a year in Chutz La'aretz. Some travel to Eretz Yisroel for every Yom Tov. Many people, as a result of modern technology, live in one country and work in another. This hardly compares with a hundred years ago when a person didn't leave the place where he lived unless there was a very pressing reason.[43]

10. *I get the idea that we really have to ask a she'eilah based on our individual circumstances but can you give me examples where the halachah is clear?*

An unmarried boy or girl studying in Eretz Yisroel for a limited amount of time, even two or three years, and plans to go back to Chutz La'aretz where their parents live, even though there is a chance that they will stay permanently in Eretz Yisroel, are considered *Bnei Chutz La'aretz* and keep two days.[44] A *chutznik* married couple living in Eretz Yisroel should ask their individual *she'eilah*. They may have plans to return home, but, on the other hand, if a source of *parnassah* would be found, they might well stay, so the *halachah* is doubtful. Someone from Eretz Yisroel who is on a *shelichus* in *Chutz La'aretz* for a limited amount of time, (as distinct from a *Chabad Shelichus* which is usually open-ended) and is contractually obliged to return to Eretz Yisroel, keeps his status as a *ben Eretz Yisroel*. Someone who moved to Chutz La'aretz for work, even if he has a vague plan to return 'at some point' will have become a *ben Chutz La'aretz*. If the situation is in between these last two cases, a *she'eilah* will have to be asked.

---

43. See *Igros Moshe* O.C. 3:74 and *Shevet Halevi* 5:64
44. This is the view of the *Igros Moshe* O.C. 2:101 but the Chazon Ish held that he should keep the second day *l'chumrah*; that is, he shouldn't do *melachos* but should say the weekday davening (with *tefillin*, except for *Chol Hamoed*).

11. *I spend the summer in Eretz Yisroel but when it gets colder I go to South Africa to enjoy the summer there. What do I do?*

If you would be spending approximately half the year in each place, you would keep *Yom Tov* according to where you are at the time.[45] However it's only really winter in Eretz Yisroel for three months so I suspect that you are in Eretz Yisroel most of the time. Therefore you should regard yourself as a *Ben Eretz Yisroel*.[46]

12. *I don't go to Chutz La'aretz for pleasure but I have a job there. I have to be there for three months a year. Is it any different for me?*

Since you 'have' to be there, if you are there over Yom Tov, you will have to keep *Yom Tov Sheini*.[47]

13. *I live most of the time in Chutz La'aretz but I am always in Eretz Yisroel for Yom Tov. I heard that I can regard myself as a ben Eretz Yisroel.*

This was indeed the view of Rav S.Z. Auerbach; even if you are in Eretz Yisroel just for *Pesach, Shavuos* and *Sukkos* and not Rosh Hashanah and Yom Kippur. But Rav Eliyashiv held that you would be a *ben Chutz La'aretz* since that is where you are most of the time. So you'll have to ask your own *Rav* what he holds.

14. *There are probably many different questions which could be asked about Yom Tov Sheini. Why don't you write a whole sefer on the subject?*

---

45. The view of Rav S.Z. Auerbach and many other *Poskim* brought in *Yom Tov Sheini Kehilchasah* 6:1
46. The view of Rav S.Z. Auerbach and Rav Y.S. Eliyashiv
47. *Yom Tov Sheini Kehilchasah* 6:2

Somebody already has.[48] If you want to see all the details, especially about *bnei Eretz Yisroel* in Chutz La'aretz and *bnei Chutz La'aretz* in Eretz Yisroel, go and learn it!

---

48. *Yom Tov Sheini Kehilchasah* by Rav Yerachmiel Fried.

Chapter Five
Cooking, Baking and Kneading

1. *Let's get back to cooking. So we're allowed to cook food on Yom Tov for Yom Tov. Are there any conditions?*

    Before I start answering, I must say something *very* important. We are not allowed to create a fire on Yom Tov. So learn this chapter bearing in mind that your electric burner must be on from before Yom Tov.[49] If you cook with gas, you either have a gas range already burning or have a flame burning from which you can light your gas.[50] Details about transferring fire and not creating a new fire and when it is permitted will be given in a later chapter.

2. *I understand. But are there conditions in connection with the leniency to cook on Yom Tov?*

    The condition, according to the Ashkenazi custom, is that we're talking about a food which wouldn't taste as good if it were cooked yesterday, as when it is cooked today.[51]

---

49. If an electric burner would be connected to a time clock so that it goes on during Yom Tov, this would also be acceptable.
50. With many modern gas ranges, lighting the gas from another light is not allowed because the gas is lit through an internal spark without an external light as explained in Chapter 7 Answer 2.
51. Rama 495:1 Mishna Berura 8.

3. *Well my wife's Shabbos food tastes great and it's cooked before Shabbos.*

    Lucky you! But I imagine you are not a connoisseur. Your expertise is more in learning a *daf Gemara*. But a connoisseur could probably tell the difference. Generally, meat, fish and kugels are tastier when fresh.

4. *Surely cholent, which is made to cook slowly over a long period, doesn't improve if it's cooked on Yom Tov, but the opposite?*

    You're right. We have to consider which foods deteriorate if cooked the day before and which not. If they wouldn't deteriorate, we are not allowed to cook them on Yom Tov.

5. *What if cooked food only stays fresh because it's in the fridge?*

    If the food stays equally good because it is refrigerated, most *Poskim* say that we have to be strict and cook it before Yom Tov.[52]

6. *But what if I didn't manage to prepare the food yesterday? Are we not allowed to have a Yom Tov seudah then?*

    If you were planning to prepare it yesterday but something unexpected happened and you could not manage, you may cook on Yom Tov in the regular way. If you just didn't manage to do it because "time ran out", you would be allowed to cook, but only in an unusual way.

7. *What do you call an unusual way?*

    Putting the pot on the cooker with your left hand if you're right-handed, or pushing it on with your elbow.

---

52. See *Shaar Hatziyun* 504:33

8.   *Are we allowed to leave the preparation deliberately and cook in an unusual way?*

There is a dispute about this but if you are short of time on Erev Yom Tov you can be lenient.[53]

9.   *What about boiling water for a drink? The water would not have deteriorated if it had been boiled before Yom Tov.*

Seeing that boiling water a day early and keeping it hot would cause the expense of having a fire underneath the kettle, this is also a reason to be lenient and allow us to boil up the water on Yom Tov.[54]

10. *What happens if I just didn't think about serving this food before Yom Tov but if I would have thought about it before Yom Tov I would have had plenty of time.*

You can also be lenient.[55]

11. *I know we're only allowed to cook for Yom Tov itself and not even for the second day Yom Tov.[56] But Moshe saw some old friends in shul and he invited them to come for the seudah tonight. How am I going to manage?*

Moshe is certainly very fortunate to be married to a big *machnisah orchim* who told him he can always invite people who may be in need of a meal, which is a wonderful *middah*. But now you need to find a solution, unless you serve sandwiches which are not so *Yomtovdik*.

---

53. *Mishnah Berurah* 495:10
54. *Yom Tov Kehilchasah* 1 Note 74
55. *Ibid.* 1:29
56. *Shulchan Aruch* O.C. 503:1 and not even during *Bein Hashemashos* (*Biur Halachah*)

If you have not yet cooked your own daytime *seudah* there are some leniencies which apply on Yom Tov but not on Shabbos. The first possibility is to add some more meat or fish[57] to the pot cooking the meat or fish for today. This extra meat or fish improves the original meat or fish, so it is allowed on Yom Tov. Practically speaking, this will give you the extra meat cooked and ready for tonight. With other foods, you can put more food into the pot than you need, as long as you prepare it all in a container and then pour it all at once into the pot.[58] Then you put the pot containing the extra food on the fire. This is regarded as *tircha achas* – one bother – and is also allowed on Yom Tov. With either of these solutions, you shouldn't say that you are really cooking for tonight although if you did, the food would not be forbidden.[59]

12. *These solutions are not going to help me because, although we have not yet eaten, I have finished all the preparations. Any other solution you might be able to think of?*

There is one other solution which although not all the *Poskim* are happy with, the *minhag* is to be lenient. That is to cook extra food of a different type than you have already prepared for the daytime meal[60] and eat some of it during the daytime *seudah*. The onlooker might think that you were cooking more food for today and there was just some leftover. But this is only permitted if you haven't eaten your daytime *seudah* yet. If you have already eaten your *seudah* this is not allowed

---

57. *Mishnah Berurah* 503:5
58. Even though *Mishna Berura* 503:14 says that the water has to be put in the pot at one time even before the pot is put on the fire and not by pouring into it several times, that is because of the great *tircha* involved in bringing water from the well, not regular preparations. (Sefer Yom Tov Kehilchaso Chapter 6 Note 29).
59. *Ibid.* 6
60. *Shaar Hatziun* 503:15

because then, even if you eat some of the food, it is clear that you were cooking for tonight.

13. *Of course nothing tastes better than fresh bread. Why don't we see more people baking bread on Yom Tov?*

In principle you are right. Certainly baking is permitted on Yom Tov for eating on Yom Tov, although turning on an oven is not allowed. Even gas ovens usually have electric components so turning them on just before you bake is not allowed. Baking needs a high temperature. Who wants to leave an oven on high in their kitchen for one or two days? A timer could help this problem but there would still be other issues, such as the problem of opening and closing the oven door, which usually affects the thermostat. Then we come to the kneading which is permitted but nowadays many people aren't accustomed to kneading by hand. They use electric mixers or bread machines which of course we may not use on Yom Tov.

If you want me to get down to the basic reason why people don't bake on Yom Tov, I would suggest that, unfortunately, a majority of women don't bake challos at all, even on Erev Shabbos or Erev Yom Tov; so what can we expect on Yom Tov? I do not mean to criticize. Women are very often "run off their feet" by their many responsibilities inside and outside the home and they don't have the time. However, baking challos at home is a beautiful and traditional custom recommended by the *Rama* 242:4, for a variety of good reasons. Those who are able to do so, *tavo aleihen brochah,* will certainly be blessed.[61]

---

61. A practical way of having more or less fresh bread for the second day Yom Tov is by baking *challos* before Yom Tov and immediately freezing them and then taking them out on the morning of the second day so that they'll be thawed by the time of the *seudah*

14. *But if I do want to bake on Yom Tov, what do I have to be careful about?*

The *Poskim*[62] say that today, when we only sift the flour to avoid little insects, we are allowed to sift the flour but with a slight difference, for instance, to sift in such a way that the flour goes onto the table rather than into a bowl. We may take out a handful or ladleful of flour from the pile of flour even though a hole would be created in the flour. We are not allowed to measure the exact amount of flour because it is not important to be so exact. We may mix the flour and water, manually, of course, in any way one wants since, unlike Shabbos, kneading is one of the permitted *melachos* of Yom Tov. If there is enough dough to separate *challah,* we have to separate *challah.* In the times of the *Beis Hamikdash* we would even be allowed to give the *challah* to a *kohen.* Today we usually burn it, but this may not be done until after Yom Tov. As we discussed earlier, we are allowed to bake only for today, not for the second day of Yom Tov and certainly not for a weekday. Baking for Shabbos on a Friday is permitted with an *eiruv tavshilin.* In the time of Chazal one could bake more than enough challos at the same time because this improved the taste of the challos one did need, but this is not relevant with our ovens and method of baking.[63]

15. *If kneading is a permitted melachah on Yom Tov, then do all the issues about preparing children's cereals and mixing mayonnaise into salads which have to be done in a special way on Shabbos, fall away?*

---

62. Be'er Moshe 8:204
63. *Shulchan Aruch* 507:6. See Mishnah Berurah 35 but the *Poskim* (Be'er Moshe 8:137) say that with our modern ovens which spread the heat equally we cannot be lenient even in an emergency.

We still have to decide whether they would be equally tasty if they were made before Yom Tov. If so, we can't make them on Yom Tov. As we mentioned above,[64] if they are equally tasty if kept refrigerated, it also has to be prepared before Yom Tov. Certain puddings[65] improve with time and therefore have to be prepared before Yom Tov. You might need to ask an expert (your wife) to see which are better fresh. But children's cereals may be made on Yom Tov in the normal weekday manner because they deteriorate if made the day before.

16. *Unfortunately we need to have a non-Jewish nurse here to look after Mom. Can she eat our Yom Tov seudah with us?*

There is a specific limitation on the leniency of cooking on Yom Tov; it is only allowed if the food is going to be eaten by a Jew.[66] In fact we are not allowed to invite a non-Jew to our home even if all the food is already cooked, as we may inadvertently cook more food for him.[67] In your case, the nurse is in your house anyway and therefore it is permitted to invite her to eat.[68] You are not allowed to cook something specific for her, but you are allowed to take her into account when preparing your meal so that there is enough for her as well.[69]

---

64. Chapter 5 Answer 5
65. US term rather than UK
66. *Shulchan Aruch* O.C. 512:1. Regarding cooking for a non-observant Jew a rav should be consulted since every case is different.
67. *Ibid.*
68. *Ibid.*
69. *Ibid.*

Chapter Six
Washing

1. *I heard that just as you can boil water to have a hot drink, you can boil up water to wash yourself. Is this correct?*

    Before answering this question, let's discuss the obligation to wash on Erev Yom Tov. As on Erev Shabbos when we wash ourselves to honor Shabbos, we should do the same on Erev Yom Tov, to honor Yom Tov.[70] We should wash our whole body or at least our face and hands in hot water.

    Concerning boiling water on Yom Tov to wash ourselves, you are correct that it is permitted, under certain conditions, but this leniency requires an explanation. Why should it be permitted? It is not *ochel nefesh* – food. There are two ways of understanding this leniency, which is based on the *Mishnah* in *Beitzah* 21b. "Beis Shammai say that we are not allowed to heat up water to wash our feet unless the water is suitable for drinking but Beis Hillel allow it and the *halachah* is like Beis Hillel."[71] The Rambam[72] says that an important physical requirement is included in the leniency of the *pasuk* which allows food and, according to the Rambam, equally vital activities such as washing are also permitted.[73]

---

70 *Mishnah Berurah* 529:3
71. *Shulchan Aruch* O.C. 511:2
72. *Hilchos Yom Tov* 1:16
73. This forces us to remember the ridiculous claims that the Jews were

Others[74] have a completely different explanation based on *Beitzah* 12a. In the *Mishnah, Beis Hillel* allow the carrying in the *reshus harabbim* of a baby for its *bris* and a *lulav* or a *Sefer Torah* which are needed on Yom Tov. The Gemara explains that *Beis Hillel* hold that when the Torah allowed us to do certain *melachos* for the purpose of *ochel nefesh,* it also allowed us to do those same *melachos* for non *ochel nefesh* purposes as long as we have a need.[75] Bringing a baby for his *bris,* bringing a *lulav* to fulfill the mitzvah or bringing a *Sefer Torah* to read from, through the *reshus harabbim,* are all allowed, just as we are allowed to carry food through the *reshus harabbim* if it is needed for eating. Similarly, since the Torah allowed us to boil water to make a hot drink on Yom Tov, we are also allowed to boil water to wash with.

2. *Great. So there's no problem in having a hot shower on Yom Tov?*

There certainly is. We are allowed to heat water only to wash our face and hands but not to have a shower or a bath. The reason for this is that we are only allowed to do the *melachos* for *ochel nefesh* or similar permitted purposes if they are *shaveh l'kol nefesh.* This means that the average person considers them a need. If they are a luxury, they are not allowed. Now washing our face and hands is certainly an important need which *halachah* requires us to do

responsible for the Black Death, the disease which killed millions of people in Europe in in the years 1347-1352. What was their evidence? That many more non-Jews died than Jews, relative to their population. Clearly we have always regarded washing as a normal and vital part of our life as human beings and Jews. Being cleaner, we were less prone to disease. Queen Elizabeth I of England once famously said that she had three baths a year, "if necessary."

74. Ran, Rashba
75. Rashi holds that the Torah allows us to do those *melachos* even if we have no need and we are forbidden only rabbinically if we have no need. Tosfos holds that if we have no need, the Torah never allowed us to do those *melachos.* This argument has repercussions in other questions as we shall see IYH.

on a daily basis. Therefore we may heat water for this purpose. But having a full bath or shower, certainly on a daily basis was not considered by *Chazal* as a need. It could be that since it is so easy for us to shower, many people do have regular showers but it is still regarded as a luxury.[76] Therefore we may only heat water to wash our face and hands, not for a shower or bath.

3. *Can we just turn on the hot tap to get hot water to wash our face and hands?*

The main problem here is not the hot water coming out, but new cold water coming into the system which will be heated, for which there may be no Yom Tov need. An electric thermostat might be activated which is a form of creating fire which is not allowed even on Yom Tov. However many opinions do allow turning on the hot tap for technical halachic reasons.[77] Some *Poskim* are *machmir.*[78] The custom, especially in *Chutz La'aretz*, seems to be lenient.[79] However, if turning on the hot water tap causes an immediate lighting of a flame or flames which go out when the tap is turned off – which is the system many people have – this is certainly not allowed.

4. *Chaim fell down in the mud and his legs are filthy. Can I clean them?*

There is a discussion in the *Poskim* whether we may heat up water to wash other limbs besides face and hands. The

76. *Chut Shoni Hilchos Yom Tov* 2:2
77. *Be'er Moshe* 1:44 *Shemiras Shabbos Kehilchasah* 2 Note 22
78. *Shevus Yitzchok* Section 6 Perek 10
79. Some creative young Jewish builders, with an eye to solving this halachic problem, now put a switch for closing the valve which allows the cold water in, in a convenient place inside the house so that the householder can easily close the valve before Yom Tov. *Yeyasher kochochom* to these builders for this great idea. However it will only help private houses which don't need so much water, not communal institutions.

conclusion of the *Biur Halachah*[80] seems to be that as long as we are talking about washing no more than half of the body, we can be lenient. So certainly in a case of need like this, it can be allowed. In fact, even if Chaim fell into mud and most of his body is dirty from the mud, there is still a strong argument to allow heating water to clean him up.[81]

5.   *Avi's having a tantrum. He needs a shower to calm him down!*

I hear the problem (just about). Is there any way we can allow this? Well, we have only said that we are not allowed to heat water for a shower because of the *melachah* of *bishul* (cooking). If we mix hot water which was heated for drinking with cold water in a *keili sheini*,[82] we have not done the *melachah* of *bishul* and you can pour the water over him according to *Sefardi* custom.[83] However even in such a case, where no *melachah* was done, or the water was heated on Erev Yom Tov, the *Ashkenazi* custom is to not allow washing the whole body together. In extenuating circumstances, though, like Avi having a tantrum, it is allowed even according to *Ashkenazi* custom.[84] It's not quite as satisfying as a shower but I think Avi will enjoy it for a change. Washing him a bit

---

80. 511 *Avol lo kol gufo.*
81. Since most people would wash themselves from actual dirt, therefore it is *shaveh l'kol nefesh*. See *Shemiras Shabbos Kehilchasah* 14: Note 25. The *Be'er Halachah* could have been talking about when someone was just sweaty but not dirty with mud etc.
82. A vessel into which hot water has been poured from a vessel that was on the stove.
83. Even according to those who say that using hot water which has been kept hot from before Shabbos is considered like water heated on Shabbos, and may not be used at all, mixing hot water with cold water in a *keli sheini* is considered like water which was heated before Shabbos and may be used even for a full wash if necessary. *Eglei Tal Ofeh* 67
84. *Mishnah Berurah* 511:18 *Biur Halachah* 326:1 *B'mayim*

at a time would also be allowed by this method.[85]You still have to be careful, however, not to do any other *melachos* like squeezing water out of a cloth or combing his hair after his wash. Using a bar of soap is not allowed. Squeezing water out of hair is not allowed[86]and we can only dab a towel on the hair to dry it.[87] Because of these reasons, the custom is not to have even a cold shower. In case of need, it is permitted if we remember not to do these other *melachos*.[88]

6.   *My neighbor says she has no time to bathe her children before Yom Tov, so she runs the bath water before Yom Tov and bathes them in the water after Yom Tov comes in. Is that allowed?*

It is not correct to arrange this as a matter of course, even according to the *Sefardi* custom.[89] If there is a special need, it can be allowed as in the previous answer.

7.   *Does all this explain why on Shabbos and Yom Tov where I live, there are three mikvahs available – a cold, warm and hot mikvah? Which one should I use?*

Let's start with the hot mikvah. According to what we have learnt, people should not be bathing in hot water. So why do some people go into the hot mikvah? The answer is that they follow an opinion[90] which holds that the prohibition is on bathing or washing. Immersion in a mikvah, according to this opinion, is neither bathing nor washing, assuming that you just go in and out, and is permitted. Although the

---

85. *Mishnah Berurah ibid.*
86. This is particularly important to remember with *peyos*.
87. *Shemiras Shabbos Kehilchasah* 14:20 Note 64
88. *Igros Moshe* Orech Chaim 4:74. *Rechitzah* 3
89. *Ibid.*
90. *Mishnah Berurah* 326:7 in the name of the *Korban Nesanel* and *Shaar Hatziyun* 5.

custom is not to immerse even in cold water, those who go to the mikvah on Shabbos and Yom Tov follow the opinion that for the purposes of *kedushah v'taharah,* it is allowed. Those who use the warm mikvah probably hold like the opinion that while immersion in hot water is forbidden according to the *halachah,* warm water, which could be described as cold water warmed up just to make it tolerable, is not forbidden.[91] One problem with these 'warm' mikvahs is that they are often hot, just not as hot as the hottest mikvah. If they are as hot as a hot bath we would have at home, they really are, halachically, the same as the hot mikvah and one hasn't gained halachically by going in this warm mikvah. If this is so, and we don't want to take advantage of the lenient opinion that considers immersing in a mikvah not under the halachic prohibition of bathing, the only option is the cold mikvah. Hence some bigger mikvahs offer these three options: hot, warm and cold.

8.   *Why do some men not go to the mikvah at all on Shabbos and Yom Tov?*

They hold that despite the additional *kedushah* and *taharah* of immersing in a mikvah, the custom of not immersing even in cold water to avoid the risk of doing *melachos,* is more important.[92] Each of the customs has an opinion to rely on and people will often just continue their family tradition. A *ba'al teshuvah* should consult his *rav.* But all those who do immerse in a mikvah on Shabbos and Yom Tov, need to be careful of *melachos* like squeezing as we mentioned above.

---

91. *Ibid.*
92. There are other possible halachic reasons not to go to the mikvah on Shabbos and Yom Tov. See *Biur Halachah 326:8 Odom.*

9.   *Are there other situations where we can heat up water?*

If we have dishes or cutlery which we dirtied on Yom Tov[93] and need to wash them for today, we may heat up the water if we need hot water to clean them properly.[94] As mentioned earlier, many *Poskim* allow turning on the hot tap even if cold water is heated up as a result. We may not wash dishes on *Yom Tov Rishon* for *Yom Tov Sheini*.[95]

10.   *Where we live it can be very cold on Pesach and Shavuos. May we turn on our central heating?*

You certainly may not turn it on because one is not allowed to create fire or electricity on Yom Tov. You may ask a non-Jew to turn it on if it is really cold. If the heating is already on, you may turn the tap to allow hot oil or water to enter the radiator. Even though this might cause more water or oil to be heated or a thermostat to go on, it is permitted.[96] Closing the tap is also permitted.[97]

---

93. If they were dirty before Yom Tov but they were left until Yom Tov, they may not be washed on Yom Tov. See *Shaar Hatziyun* 507:63
94. *Rama* 511:2. If they can be cleaned equally well with cold water, we should not heat up water (*Chut Shoni*).
95. *Shulchan Aruch* O.C. 503:1
96. *Shemiras Shabbos Kehilchasah* 2:7 *Hilchos Chag B'Chag* 10:6. A minority view does not allow this.
97 *Shemiras Shabbos Kehilchasah* 23:19

Chapter Seven
Lighting Fires

1. *If the Torah allows us to cook on Yom Tov, we must be allowed to light a fire. Otherwise how can we cook?*

I'm afraid there is a flaw in your reasoning. We mentioned earlier that we may not do a *melachah* on Yom Tov even in order to prepare food if it could have been done equally effectively before Yom Tov. In this case, also, we could have lit the fire before Yom Tov and merely transferred the flame without creating a new flame.[98] We are allowed to cook on a fire but we are only allowed to transfer a flame from a pre-lit fire or a flame. Creating a new fire on Yom Tov is definitely not allowed.[99]

2. *Do we have to leave the gas of the stove lit from before Yom Tov or can we just leave a small candle burning which is a lot cheaper?*

A small candle or any lit flame is enough. Indeed most families light a 26 hour candle before Yom Tov so that they will have a flame to light from in cases of need over Yom Tov. Where two days Yom Tov are being kept obviously the candle will be twice as big. However, nowadays, even this is often not allowed because many modern gas ranges ignite a spark

98. *Mishnah Berurah* 502:1
99. *Shulchan Aruch* O.C. 502:1

before any gas is released. Therefore, with these modern gas ranges, the gas will have to be lit, at least on a low light, from before Yom Tov.

3.   *Can my neighbor and I share a flame?*

In principle yes but if you will have to go outside your front door or even into a drafty corridor, this won't be a good idea because the candle is likely to blow out.

4.   *In the evening, can I take a flame from the Yom Tov candles?*

Yes, since the Yom Tov lights are to give benefit to the house, it is not regarded as disrespectful to use their flame for another Yom Tov need.[100] However it is better to use this leniency only if there is no other option since some *Poskim*[101] are unsure about it.

5.   *May I light a match from a flame and take the match to light another flame?*

Yes.

6.   *May I put a match against an electric burner so that the match lights?*

Unless the burner is red hot, it is considered creating a fire and is not allowed.[102]

7.   *You said in Chapter Six that since we can cook food to eat and boil water to drink, we can cook or boil for other purposes as well. Does*

100. *Be'er Moshe* 8:179, Rav S.Z. Auerbach brought in S.S.K. 44 Note 35
101. *Chut Shoni* 1:1
102. *Ibid.* Only if it would be red-hot would most *Poskim* allow it. *Igros Moshe Y.D.* 2:75 D.H *Ubedavar lehadlik*

this apply to lighting a fire for non-ochel nefesh needs as well?

Yes, we can light a fire for warmth or to see with. Lighting Yom Tov candles, even if they aren't needed to see with, is allowed because the more light, the more *simchah.*

8. *So I don't need to light my Yom Tov candles before Yom Tov comes in as I do on Shabbos?*

Correct, but it is preferable to light before *shekiah* in honor of Yom Tov.[103]

9. *May we light before shekiah on the first day of Yom Tov for the second evening of Yom Tov?*

No, on the second night of Yom Tov you should light only after it is completely dark.[104]

10. *What happens if the second night of Yom Tov is a Shabbos?*

It is better to light just before *shekiah* in order to benefit from the light before nightfall.[105] If you have electric lights, if you have a time-clock, you can set it before Yom Tov so the lights go off for a short time just then, so that you will benefit from the Yom Tov lights. If you do not have a time-clock, or you

---

103. To honor Yom Tov in the correct way. *Hilchos Yom Tov* of Rav Eliyashiv. The Rambam *Hilchos Shabbos* (30:5) writes "On returning from shul he should find the table ready and the light lit." and the same applies on Yom Tov (*Hilchos Yom Tov* 6:16). However some people have the *minhag* to light after nightfall so as not to make a mistake and light on the first day of Yom Tov for the second day. Each person should follow their family custom.

104. *Ibid.* We may clean out any remaining wax before putting new candles or, for those who use oil lights, clear away the old wick. We can put a new wick through the hole in the wick holder but we are not allowed to make a hole if there is none.

105. *Chut Shoni* 1:1 This the case, *lechatchila,* even if we have made *eiruv tavshilin,* for the same reason that we should cook early enough on *Yom Tov* which falls on *Erev Shabbos* that guests might come and have benefit from the cooked food.

have to leave for shul some time before *shekiah*, you should still light the Shabbos candles despite the fact that the room is light from daylight or electric lights because it can still be argued that candles increase *simchah* somewhat even during the day.

11. *Can we use a flame to light candles for the daytime seudah?*

If the room is dark and candles would brighten the room it is allowed. [106]

12. *At a seudas mitzvah like a bris we usually have candles on the table. Is this allowed on Yom Tov?*

Yes. [107]

13. *I have a yahrzeit on the second day of Yom Tov. Can I light a yahrzeit candle?*

There is a question about this. It is a worthy *minhag* but is it a need? The best solution is to light a 48-hour candle before Yom Tov. Failing this you could light your candle in your shul where there is a mitzvah to have lights. If this is not feasible, you can light it at home near your table because extra light, at least during the night, is always useful.

14. *When Yom Tov falls on Motza'ei Shabbos may we light a special havdalah light which is only for the mitzvah of havdalah?*

The *Poskim* grapple with the question of whether the custom of lighting a multi-wicked candle constitutes enough of a Yom Tov need. Holding the flames of the two Yom Tov candles together is also controversial. This will anyway not work

106. *Mishnah Berurah* 514:30
107. *Ibid.*

with oil lights which many people use nowadays. So is there any way of fulfilling all opinions? Fortunately, one can now buy standard size candles with double wicks or a small multi-wicked *havdalah* candle which solves the problem. We can light regular Yom Tov lights with oil, if that is our custom, but for this night put one of these double- or multi-wicked candles on the table in a candlestick and light them. The flames join together constituting the *medurah* – the larger flame which we need for *havdalah* but last throughout the meal adding to the light and joy of our Yom Tov table. This fulfills all opinions.

15. *I see people smoking on Yom Tov but you said before that we are only allowed to do melachos which are shaveh lekol nefesh – regular activities for regular people. Today less than one sixth of the population smoke. Is it still allowed?*

There are a number of problems with smoking on Yom Tov including lighting, extinguishing and erasing besides the general prohibition of doing something injurious to health. Heavy smokers, because they are addicted, will claim that they suffer considerably when they don't smoke and for them it is an important need. Most *Poskim* do not agree with this. I will just quote Rav Elyashiv:

"Nowadays when all the doctors agree that smoking is very bad for one's health and many people have given up smoking because of this, smoking is forbidden on Yom Tov because of a fear that it is not *shaveh l'kol nefesh* and forbidden according to the Torah." This is the widely held opinion.

16. *You mentioned that creating a fire on Yom Tov is not allowed. Is this prohibited according to the Torah or rabbinically?*

Most opinions hold that the prohibition is rabbinic.[108] In situations of emergency this might enable your rav to allow asking a non-Jew.[109]

17. *If creating a fire is only a rabbinic prohibition, is there more reason to allow opening a fridge on Yom Tov than on Shabbos?*

There are a number of issues concerning opening a fridge. Modern fridges have a number of electronically controlled functions which begin to work as soon as the door is opened. The most obvious one is the light, which is certainly forbidden even on Yom Tov. Some opinions hold that creating an electric current involves the *melachah* of building for which there is no leniency on Yom Tov.[110] Therefore it is better to have a fridge which has a Shabbos mode[111] and use it for Yom Tov as well. If you are sure that the only issue is the motor going on in response to warm air which doesn't happen straight away, opening the door when the motor is on is allowed on Shabbos and Yom Tov. Some would allow it even if the motor is not on, on Shabbos and certainly on Yom Tov. However most modern fridges have many other issues besides the motor so, in practice, we should be as strict on Yom Tov as on Shabbos.

---

108. See *Biur Halachah* 502:1 and *Yom Tov Kehilchasah* 22:4
109. Like other rabbinic prohibitions. See *Shulchan Aruch* O.C. 307:5. If a non-Jew did a *melachah* which we would not be allowed to ask him to do, we are not allowed to have any benefit from that *melachah* until the end of that Yom Tov (including the second day and including Shabbos if it falls immediately after Yom Tov) and we have to add on the amount of time it took for the non-Jew to do the *melachah*. If there is a special need, a rav should be consulted. See *Shulchan Aruch* 515 and commentaries. The same applies if the non-Jew brought something from outside the *techum*.
110. *Chazon Ish.*
111. It is important to note that some Shabbos modes function according to the stricter opinion of the Chazon Ish; others function according to lenient opinions. Those who are usually careful to eat food which is *mehadrin* should also buy a fridge which has a *mehadrin* Shabbos mode.

Chapter Eight
Extinguishing

1. *Are we never allowed to extinguish a fire on Yom Tov?*

   If the extinguishing is non-food related, it is not allowed.

2. *Are you telling me that even if my house was burning down, I would not be allowed to put it out?*

   In a built-up area, we have to assume that allowing a fire to rage would be a possible danger to life in the houses nearby. If so, it is permitted, even to call the fire department. This is permitted even on Shabbos.

3. *You mean if our holiday house which is not near any other house is on fire, we can't put it out?*

   If you would have nowhere else to eat your Yom Tov *seudah*, it would be permitted. Some *Poskim* allow you to call the (non-Jewish) fire department on Yom Tov to save you the loss of money, even if you do have somewhere else to eat.[112]

4. *Is there another case when extinguishing is allowed?*

   When your food is getting burnt.

112. Netta Gavriel 21:23

5.   *But why can't I just take the food away from the fire to prevent it from being burnt?*

This refers to a case where the food isn't cooked yet.

6.   *But why shouldn't I light another flame to cook the food?*

You have an electric cooker which we are not allowed to light on Yom Tov.

7.   *When I light my gas range, at first there is big flame which must be lowered to the level needed. Am I allowed to do this?*

Since this is the normal way this range works, it is allowed.[113]

8.   *My gas range has electric ignition. Can I use it?*

No.

9.   *What if the bedroom light is on and it is disturbing?*

You can call in a non-Jew and say that the light has been left on and it disturbs you. He should understand that you want him to turn the light off. This is permitted even on Shabbos. If there is no non-Jew and it is the second night of Yom Tov, you should ask your *Rav* if you may be lenient.

10.   *Someone told me that when you light a candle from an existing candle, you should take the unlit candle to the old light rather than the other way round because of extinguishing. What does he mean?*

If you take an existing candle to light a new candle, you will inevitably hold the original candle in a slanting position. On

113. *Sefer Yom Tov Kehilchasah* 11:17

the original candle there will always be liquid wax which will drip off as you light the new candle. This removal of the liquid wax from the candle will cause the candle to go out sooner. This is not allowed because of extinguishing.[114] If you put the unlit candle into the flame of the old candle, this will not happen. Even though this extinguishing is not our intention, it is better to avoid it.

11. *Is there anything else we need to avoid in order not to extinguish on Yom Tov?*

When you are carrying a candle from place to place, you should avoid windy places or fans which could blow out the flame.[115]

114. *Yom Tov Kehilchasah* 11:30
115. *Rama* 514:3

CHAPTER NINE
Carrying

1. *You mentioned earlier that we are allowed to carry on Yom Tov. I presume you mean both from a reshus harabim to a reshus hayachid and the opposite and also to carry four amos in the reshus harabbim.*

    Yes.

2. *Does that include any type of food, including food which most people don't eat, like vegetables out of season which are expensive?*

    I think that you're worried about the condition of being *shaveh l'kol nefesh* – something which the average person enjoys, and not just very pampered people. But this is not a problem here because it is not just pampered people who enjoy such a fruit; we all would. It just happens to be expensive.[116]

3. *I need to take pills every day. Is this considered shaveh l'kol nefesh to allow me to carry them in the street seeing that anybody could get my condition?*

    There is a dispute about this but the final *halachah* is that a medical need is not considered *shaveh l'kol nefesh*[117] and may

---

116. *Mishnah Berurah* 511:25
117. *Chut Shoni* Perek 10. *Shemiras Shabbos Kehilchasah* 14: Note 25

not be carried in a *reshus harabbim* on Yom Tov. However on a road which is a *karmalis* or even a doubtful *reshus harabbim*[118] like most of our main roads, you can be lenient.[119] If there is a reliable *eiruv* it is certainly allowed.

4. *What about carrying a pack of cigarettes?*

See Chapter Seven, Question 15.

5. *My cousin invited us to come on Yom Tov and I offered to bring a cake. Do I have to take it before Yom Tov to avoid carrying on Yom Tov?*

Although other *melachos* should be done before Yom Tov if nothing would be lost thereby, carrying food in the street does not have this requirement.[120]

6. *I see people carrying all sorts of things on Yom Tov like tissues, machzorim or lulavim. Are there no restrictions?*

We are allowed to carry only what we need or might need. For example, an old tissue which we may have left in our pocket should be discarded before we go outside.[121]

7. *I have a bag of tissues and I certainly won't need all of them. Do I have to count out the maximum number I might need and leave the rest at home?*

---

118. Because 600,000 people do not go on it every day.
119. *Chut Shoni* 10
120. *Mishnah Berurah* 498:10
121. If a person uses a tissue in the street and it is no longer usable, in principle it should be thrown away but seeing that this could well cause a serious *chillul Hashem*, one should put it back into one's pocket where there are other tissues and rely on the Yom Tov leniency of *marbeh b'shiurim*. (Similar to the *limud zechus* mentioned in *Shut Eretz Zvi Teshuva* 75)

If all the tissues are in one bag or even in one pocket, we are allowed to take out more than we need.[122]

8. *Some men carry their tallis home and some men continue to wear it. Why are there arguments about everything?*

There is no argument. Those who left their *tallis* in shul from before Yom Tov and therefore are obviously not worried about losing it, may not carry their *tallis* in the street. Those who just took it on Yom Tov morning may carry it back. The same applies to *machzorim*. This falls into the category of *hitiru sofon mishum techiloson*. Chazal allowed people who are worried about losing these items which are required for a mitzvah to bring them home because otherwise they may not want to take them to shul.[123]

9. *What about the flag that Yossele took to shul for Simchas Torah? Can he bring it home?*

I'm sure Yossele really enjoyed joining the *hakafos* with his flag. It was his *simchas Yom Tov* as well as *kovod HaTorah*. But he can only bring it home if he is still going to play with it at home.[124]

10. *Can I carry my house key in my pocket?*

If you need the key to get into your house and there is no-one you could leave the key with, you can certainly take it with

122. *Igros Moshe* O.C. 2:103 *Chut Shoni Perek* 6 This *halachah* of *ribui b'shiurim* comes from the leniency to cook more water than one needs if no extra act is done. The *Poskim* apply this principle to carrying as well.
123. *Mishnah Berurah* 518:7
124. The leniency mentioned before of *hitiru sofon mishum techiloson* only applies to a clear mitzvah like *tallis* or *machzor,* but not to just anything which gives a person *simchah* (Rav Asher *shlita*)

you. If you are not planning to return home until after Yom Tov, you should not carry the key in your pocket[125] but rather use a Shabbos belt. In an emergency when you need to go out until after Yom Tov, do not have a Shabbos belt and are afraid that your unlocked home might be burgled, there are lenient opinions.[126]

11. *Does this mean that I shouldn't bring my towel home from the mikvah even if it might get lost?*

Since the only reason to bring it home is the risk of financial loss, it is not allowed, as in Answer 10. Although going to the mikvah for additional sanctity is regarded by many as an important *hanhagah*, and in answer 8 we allowed a *tallis* or *machzor* to be carried home because of *hitiru sofon mishum haschalasan*, this was because the *tallis* and *machzor* are really required whereas going to the mikvah is not obligatory.[127] So, unless you need the towel at home during Yom Tov or you want to wrap it round your neck like a scarf, you'll have to leave your towel there. Due to these considerations, most mikvahs provide towels for all those who need them.

12. *Can I take a trash can outside?*

A trash can is generally *muktzeh* and shouldn't be moved at all. If it smells, it may be moved but, if possible, it should be left within one's *reshus hayochid.* If the only way to be rid of the odor is to take it outside into the *reshus harabbim,* you may do so.[128]

---

125. *Mishnah Berurah* 518:6
126. *Rama* 518:1. Avoiding worry that he might suffer financially is also regarded as a Yom Tov need. Perhaps we can add the possibility that his plans will change and he will need to go back to his home before the end of Yom Tov.
127. And even if it were a mitzvah to *tovel* in a mikvah it is not a mitzvah to get dried.
128. *Mishnah Berurah* 514:7. We see there that even though there is no positive result from extinguishing but merely preventing something undesirable, it is

13. *Our non-Jewish cleaning lady left her coat in our house and she
     probably needs it. Can I take it to her house?*

     As we mentioned above[129] we are not allowed to do a *melachah*
     for a non-Jew on Yom Tov so this won't be allowed.

14. *I want to take the children to the park. Obviously I'll need to take
     the baby. Is this allowed?*

     This is regarded as *simchas Yom Tov* and it is allowed. But if you
     take the baby in a carriage or stroller, remove any items which
     you won't need before you go out. Enjoy!

15. *Malka is in hospital and it's Rosh Hashanah. May I take a shofar
     when I visit so I can blow for her?*

     Women are not obliged to hear the shofar in the same way as men
     are, but it is still a mitzvah when they hear it, so you can take the
     shofar with you.[130] The same applies to a *lulav* on Succos. We can
     take a shofar or *lulav* through the street even for Sefardi women
     who don't say a *brochah* on a *mitzvas asei shehazman grama*.[131]

16. *Zeidy needs a cane when he walks in the street. Is this allowed?*

     If he really needs it to stop himself from falling, it is allowed.
     Otherwise not, even if there is an *eiruv*.[132] If he can walk without
     a cane but because of ice or uneven surfaces he is liable to fall,
     he may also take his cane.[133] We have heard of old people who

---

allowed to do the *melachah*. We can apply this to the question of taking out
the trash where there is no alternative. *Sefer Yom Tov Kehilchaso* 13

129. See Chapter Five Answer 6
130. *Igros Moshe* O.C. 3:94
131. *Ibid.*
132. *Mishnah Berurah* 522:2
133. See a dispute on this point in *Mishnah Berurah* 301: 65 in *Hilchos Shabbos*
where *Mishnah Berurah* is inclined to be strict but on Yom Tov we can be

have gone without a cane and unfortunately fallen and hurt themselves, so we have to be careful with this *halachah*. It applies only in a *reshus harabbim* or *karmelis* but not *chatzer me'ureves* (a jointly owned yard where an *eiruv* was made).[134]

17. *Why is using an unnecessary cane not allowed even if there is an eiruv?*

The reason is that it is regarded as *uvdin d'chol* – a weekday activity – and not because of carrying on Yom Tov, so an *eiruv* doesn't help.

18. *Can I push him in a wheelchair?*

Certainly.[135]

19. *And pushing a young child in a stroller?*

Also permitted.[136]

20. *What about carrying a machzor to shul on the first day of Yom Tov only for use on the second day?*

This is not allowed because you are not going to use the *machzor* today and also because of the prohibition of *hachanah* – preparing for the second day or for after Yom Tov. This is not allowed even if there is an *eiruv*.[137]

21. *I need my machzor for Maariv which starts at nightfall. How am I going to get it there?*

more lenient (Rav Tuvia Dinkel *shlita*).
134. *Ibid.*
135. *Yom Tov Kehilchasah* 13:62
136. Ibid. Note 199
137. *Mishnah Berurah* 503:1

One option is to arrange for a *machzor* to be in shul for you, either from before Yom Tov or by leaving the *machzor* which you used in the morning in shul. The other option is for the shul to start *Maariv* later to give people time to bring their *machzorim* after nightfall.

22. *Am I allowed to carry anything during bein hashemashos, even something I need later like a tissue? Seeing that we don't know when the new day really begins, isn't there a danger that I am carrying for the next day?*

    Indeed carrying a handkerchief which you don't need until later will not be allowed but if you have cold and might need it at any time, it will be allowed. If you are carrying a sefer and are reading from the sefer as you are going along, it will also be permitted.[138]

23. *Are we allowed to go outside the techum on Yom Tov?*

    No.[139]

---

138. *Haga'as* Rebbe Akiva Eger 495
139. *Shulchan Aruch* O.C. 397:3

Chapter Ten
Borer - Separating

1. *Borer is a complex melachah on Shabbos. Is it any easier on Tom Tov?*

I'm afraid it is quite complicated on Yom Tov as well, especially if you want to fulfill all opinions.

Although we will try and go through these *halachos* clearly, it would be better to first go through Chapter Twenty about *borer* in my *sefer, Do You Know Hilchos Shabbos?*

2. *Okay. I've been through borer on Shabbos. Is it more lenient on Yom Tov?*

In certain ways, yes. Let's take *borer* with two items of food first. On Yom Tov, if you have a bag containing mostly oranges and just a few apples and you want to serve the oranges but not the apples, not only may we take out the apples, we *must* take out the apples because this is less work. On Shabbos, we have to take the oranges and leave the apples.[140]

3. *Is this allowed only for immediate use or can it be done for later that day?*

According to the *halachah,* it may be done for any time on that

140. *Shulchan Aruch O.C. 510:2, Mishnah Berurah 6*

day of Yom Tov but some are *mehader* to do it only for now or at the latest, for the next meal but not on the night of Yom Tov for the next afternoon.[141]

4. *Some of the fruit in the bowl has gone bad. I only want to serve the good ones. Does the same halachah apply?*

Yes. Even if the fruit was so bad that it was inedible and on Shabbos would be *muktzeh,* on Yom Tov we have to take the bad fruit away.

5. *Unfortunately most of the fruit has gone bad. What do I do now?*

Now you have to take the good ones away because it is less work than taking the majority of bad fruit away.

6. *Should I separate the fruit before Yom Tov, if I can?*

Yes. If you remember from the *halachos* of cooking on Yom Tov,[142] we are only allowed to cook on Yom Tov if the food would have been inferior if it were cooked before Yom Tov. If it could been cooked just as easily and without deteriorating before Yom Tov, we may not cook it on Yom Tov. The same applies to other *melachos* which are permitted on Yom Tov – like *borer*; we have to do it before Yom Tov if possible. Only if we forgot or we didn't have time or maybe in this case when the fruit went bad on Yom Tov itself, are we permitted to do *borer* on Yom Tov. However it can still be done as on Shabbos, taking what we want from what we don't want for immediate use.

---

141. Because of the opinion of the Rashba who does not allow *borer* even on Yom Tov unless it is just before use. *Taz* 510:4 brought in *Biur Halacha* 510:2 However see *Yom Tov Kehilchasah* 8 Note 15 in the name of the Me'iri that even according to the Rashba we can prepare for the next meal.
142. Above Chapter 5 Question 3

7. *I need to wash the fruit. Can I wash it on Yom Tov?*

If the fruit is clean but you just want to wash it again for extra cleanliness, this is permitted. If it the fruit is soiled and inedible without being washed, you can put the dirty fruit under running tap water to clean it.[143] However we are not allowed to put the dirty fruit or vegetables into a bowl of water for the dirt to come off.[144] We also may not soak lettuce in water in order to clean and check it for possible bugs.[145]

8. *May we peel the apples with a peeler?*

Household implements like potato peelers, slotted spoons, colanders, strainers etc. are all permitted on Yom Tov.[146]

9. *I know that on Shabbos we may not separate knives, spoons and forks if they are mixed together unless it is just before the meal. Is this an issue on Yom Tov as well?*

Concerning Yom Tov night the question is whether the table could have been set before Yom Tov. Probably the answer is yes. Therefore setting the evening meal should be done either before Yom Tov or just before the meal like on Shabbos because as we have mentioned earlier, even a *melachah* which is allowed on Yom Tov should be done before Yom Tov, if it could have been done without a loss. You can set the table for the daytime *seudah* in advance according to all opinions, because we said[147] that on Yom Tov any time after the previous meal is considered "immediately before."

---

143. *Yom Tov Kehilchasah* 8:8
144. *Ibid.*
145. *Ibid.*
146. *Biur Halacha* 510:4 s.v. *mutar litein.*
147. Above 3A

10. *Taking bones out of fish is another halachic minefield on Shabbos. Is it easier on Yom Tov?*

Yes, on Yom Tov it is permitted because it is for eating straight away and it could not be done before Yom Tov without spoiling the appearance of the fish.[148]

11. *Ugh! A fly has fallen in my soup. How do I get it out?*

It is better to take it out together with some of the soup as on Shabbos.[149]

12. *What about borer with non-food items?*

Many *Poskim* hold that for non-food items, the *halachah* is the same on Yom Tov as on Shabbos[150] but some are lenient.[151]

148. *Yom Tov Kehilchasah* 8 Note 64 in the name of Rav Eliyashiv.
149. *Mishnah Berurah* 506:12
150. *Mishnah Berurah* 518:1 that we only say *mitoch* in *melachos* of *hotza'ah, havara, shechita, afia* and *bishul.*
151. *Shevet Halevi* 1:79

Chapter Eleven
Tochein – Grinding

1. *Is the melachah of tochein permitted on Yom Tov?*

   It is a *melachah* which in some cases could be forbidden according to the Torah and in other cases completely permitted. We need to learn the details very carefully.

2. *In which cases might it be forbidden according to the Torah?*

   Grinding wheat in an industrial mill to make flour is forbidden by the Torah according to some opinions. This is even if you need the flour to bake bread on Yom Tov which is allowed as we saw earlier.[152] If it is for after Yom Tov, as it invariably is in a commercial mill, it will be forbidden according to the Torah according to many more opinions.

3. *For most of us, questions of tochein involve cutting up vegetables, mashing potatoes during our Yom Tov seudah and mashing fruit to give to children. Are these permitted or not?*

   Let's discuss one thing at a time.

___

152. 5:13

4. *I usually serve carrot salad, tomato and cucumber salad, cabbage salad etc. They are obviously better and fresher if I prepare them just before the meal.*

A salad which is significantly better when fresh, can be made on Yom Tov rather than Erev Yom Tov and may be cut up into small pieces in the normal way.[153]

5. *What about a type of vegetable salad which would stay fresh in a fridge but would deteriorate if it were left out of the fridge?*

This is considered as if it could have been made before Yom Tov and is only permitted in an unusual way.[154] This could be achieved by cutting the vegetables in a way that the pieces fall onto a table rather than into a bowl or onto a napkin rather than onto a plate. If you usually use a machine to cut vegetables during the week, using a knife is regarded as an unusual way.

6. *What is the point of doing things in an unusual way?*

There is a lot of Talmudic background which results in this halachic conclusion.[155] One reason mentioned in the early *Poskim* is to remind ourselves not to prepare anything for after Yom Tov, even for the second day Yom Tov which is strictly forbidden.[156]

7. *What about mashing avocado?*

If you need it for the first day of Yom Tov, it would probably

153. *Mishnah Berurah* 504:19. However for the evening *seudah* the salad could have been prepared before Yom Tov without any deterioration, so it will require a change in the normal way of preparation as will be explained.
154. *Shaar Hatziyun* 504:33
155. See *Beitzah* 12a
156. *Mishnah Berurah* 504:11

be fine kept in the fridge covered by Saran Wrap (cling film).[157] Therefore if you didn't do it before Yom Tov, you should mash it in an unusual way, e.g. with a spoon or the handle of the fork. If you need it for the second day of Yom Tov, it would have deteriorated by then so on the second day, you can mash it in the usual way.

8. *Avi is really particular that his mashed banana is up to scratch. Can I mash it in the regular way?*

I agree with Avi. Bananas don't stay so good even if kept in a fridge so you can mash them in the regular way on Yom Tov.

9. *I have a standard Yom Tov recipe which involves cooking potatoes on Yom Tov morning, mashing the potatoes, mixing them with gravy and serving them with meat. The kids love it. I can't mash the potatoes before Yom Tov because they weren't cooked yet. Is this okay?*

Let's assume that potatoes would deteriorate significantly if they were mashed before Yom Tov and therefore it is allowed, even with a fork in the usual way. But I may have news for you. Mashing cooked potatoes, if they have been very well-softened by the cooking process, is permitted even on Shabbos and certainly on Yom Tov.[158] On Yom Tov we can be even more lenient in that on Shabbos a potato masher is not allowed but on Yom Tov it is.

10. *If we may use implements, may I use a grater to prepare Avi's apple?*

---

157. A practical point: if you add in a small amount of lemon juice, the avocado keeps its green color.
158. *Shemiras Shabbos Kehilchasah* 6:10

Since the apple would definitely deteriorate significantly if you grated it before Yom Tov, you can grate it even in the usual way.

11. *What about foods which do not grow in the ground, like meat or cheese?*

To grate items which don't grow in the ground without using a special implement is permitted on Yom Tov as it is on Shabbos. On Shabbos a special implement like a grater or grinder is definitely not allowed. On Yom Tov it may be used but only in an unusual way, since meat, fish or cheese wouldn't deteriorate. Grate or grind onto a napkin or onto the table as we said before or by holding the grater the other way around.[159]

12. *Does the same apply if the meat was only cooked on Yom Tov?*

No. If it were only cooked on Yom Tov, even a grinder can be used in the usual way.

13. *Hey, we forgot to grate the chrein before the Seder. Can we do it now?*

Yes but in an unusual way. Enjoy your Seder.

14. *I have a recipe using broken matzah, cream cheese with cinnamon and other flavorings. The kids love it and they even make it themselves. Can they do it on Yom Tov?*

Sure. Since matzah was already ground, there is no prohibition of breaking it up even on Shabbos and certainly on Yom Tov.[160]

---

159. On Shabbos there is no leniency to grind meat even in an unusual way (*Shulchan Aruch* O.C. 321:10).
160. Rama 504:3

Sounds like it would be nice for Shavuos as well as Pesach. Don't forget to invite me!

15. *I know that the prohibition on Shabbos against taking medicines was originally made because people might grind herbs to make medicines. Since tochen is sometimes permitted on Yom Tov, does this make a difference to the halachos of taking medicines on Yom Tov?*

There is some discussion in the *Poskim* on this point for the reason you mention but the conclusion is that the *halachos* are the same on Shabbos and Yom Tov.[161] However on the second day of Yom Tov, excluding the second day of Rosh Hashanah, we are allowed to take medicines if we are in some degree of pain as we explained above Chapter 4 Answer 2.[162]

161. *Mishnah Berurah* 532:5
162. *Rama* 496:2 and see *Mishnah Berurah* 496: 5

Chapter Twelve
Muktzeh

1. *Seeing that the halachos of Yom Tov are more lenient than those of Shabbos, obviously the halachos of muktzeh will be more lenient. Aren't I right?*

    It's good you bought this *sefer* because you will be surprised to learn that in some areas, the *halachos* of *muktzeh* on Yom Tov are stricter than on Shabbos.

2. *Why?*

    Because Chazal in their wisdom perceived that people might have less respect for Yom Tov because of the leniencies concerning food preparation so they strengthened Yom Tov in people's eyes by making some *halachos* of *muktzeh* stricter on Yom Tov than on Shabbos.[163]

3. *With which halachos were Chazal stricter for Yom Tov than for Shabbos?*

    In the area called *nolad* which means literally 'newly born.'

4. *Is a newborn baby muktzeh???*

---

163. *Beitzah* 2b

Of course not, but a newborn calf is and so is a new-laid egg.[164]
These are *muktzeh* on Shabbos also.

5. *If they are born or laid on the first day of Yom Tov are they permitted on the second day?*

Yes, but not on the second day of Rosh Hashanah.[165]

6. *What is an example of nolad which is permitted on Shabbos but not allowed on Yom Tov?*

After you have eaten a portion of chicken, there will probably be bones on your plate. If the bones have enough meat on them that you might decide still to finish them off, they are not *muktzeh*. If there is no meat on them, since your neighborhood dogs would still be interested in them, they are not *muktzeh* on Shabbos. But concerning Yom Tov, since on Erev Yom Tov the chicken was set aside for people to eat, their availability for animals is a newly created situation, they fall in the category of *nolad* and are *muktzeh*. The same applies to orange peels; even though they are now suitable for animals to eat, they are *muktzeh*.[166]

7. *So how are we supposed to get rid of them?*

If they are still on your plate, you can take the plate away from the table and discard the bones or peel into the trash. If they are on the tablecloth, and you need that area of the tablecloth where the bones are,[167] you can push them onto a plate using

164. *Shulchan Aruch* O.C. 513:1 and 8.
165. *Ibid.* 513:5
166. *Mishnah Berurah* 495:17. If there are no animals in the vicinity to which the bones or peel could have been given, they are *muktzeh* even on Shabbos.
167. *Mishnah Berurah* 308:115

a piece of cutlery and take the plate away. If there are a lot of bones or peel and it is very unpleasant to look at, they may be moved under the category of *muktzeh* called *graf shel re'i.*[168]

8. *If Yom Tov falls on Shabbos do we have to follow the stricter Yom Tov halachah or can we be lenient as on Shabbos?*[169]

There is a dispute in this matter between the *Poskim*[170] so it is better to apply the stricter Yom Tov *halachah*, seeing that, anyway, we can push the *muktzeh* onto a plate with a knife etc.

9. *Are there any other examples of nolad which are muktzeh on both Shabbos and Yom Tov?*

Water dripping from an air conditioning outlet which has just condensed from the air in your home is *muktzeh* because of *nolad* both on Shabbos and Yom Tov.

10. *Is rain nolad?*

No, because we assume that the rainwater existed from before Shabbos.

11. *What about ice that has just melted?*

Unlike Shabbos when we are careful to put ice cubes into a pitcher of water rather than into an empty pitcher, on Yom Tov we do not have to be concerned, according to most opinions.[171] However seeing that there is a stricter opinion and it is easy to

168. Ibid
169. *Shemiras Shabbos Kehilchasa* 21:8
170. See *Yom Tov Kehilchasah* 20 Note 5
171. *Shvus Yitzchak inyanei Yom Tov* in the name of Rav Eliyashiv and *Shemiras Shabbos Kehilchasah* Chapter 12 Note 31 in the name of Rav Shlomo Zalman Auerbach.

put water into a pitcher and then put the ice in, it is better to do it that way.

12.   *Is this very complicated or is it just me?*

It's complicated.

13.   *In which cases are the halachos of muktzeh on Yom Tov more lenient than Shabbos?*

They fall into two main categories. One is those items which are *muktzeh* on Shabbos because they are normally used for a *melachah* which is not allowed on Shabbos. If this *melachah* is allowed on Yom Tov, the item is automatically not *muktzeh*. This category includes items such as pots and pans for cooking, candles, candlesticks, domestic graters and peelers etc. Matches may be moved if you need then to transfer a flame for a Yom Tov need and there is no alternative; otherwise matches are *muktzeh* because their primary function is creating a flame which is not allowed on Yom Tov.[172] Raw food is also not *muktzeh* since it may be cooked. The second category contains items which are normally *muktzeh* even on Yom Tov but because they happen to be in the way when preparing food, they may be moved. See an example in the next question.

14.   *Unfortunately, we had to come inside from our Sukkah because of a sudden downpour. But Mommy had left her handbag full of muktzeh items on the dining room table. Can we move it?*

This is an example of the second category. Seeing that you need the table to eat on you can take the handbag away.

---

172. Sefer *Yom Tov Kehilchasah* 20:25

15. *Can you give some more examples?*

Opening a silverware drawer which is also used as a stationery drawer, or removing a log which has fallen against the door of my house preventing me from coming in to have my Yom Tov *seudah* are permitted on Yom Tov.

16. *Are there any more examples of cases in category one or two?*

You have to think and tell me![173]

17. *We mentioned earlier that some Rishonim say that washing our face and hands and other essential needs are also regarded as ochel nefesh. May I move muktzeh from the sink so that I can wash my hands?*

Yes.[174]

18. *Is food muktzeh on Yom Kippur?*

No, since it is permitted for young children.[175]

19. *Are gebrochts (anything cooked with matzo meal), which some people are machmir not to eat on Pesach, muktzeh for those who are machmir?*

No, since even those who are *machmir* agree that it is not *chametz* according to the strict *halachah* because they do eat *gebrochts* on the eighth day.[176]

---

173. What about *sechach* falling down onto your table in the sukkah which you need to move before you can sit down there for your *seudah*?
174. *Shemiras Shabbos Kehilchasah* Perek 21, Note 6 in the name of Rav S.Z. Auerbach
175. *Rama* 612:10
176. *Chazon Ish* O.C. 49:16.

20. *What about a shofar or the arba minim after they have been used to do the mitzvah?*

They are not *muktzeh* since they could still be used for someone who hasn't done the mitzvah.[177]

21. *Since we don't use them for the mitzvah on Shabbos, are they muktzeh when Yom Tov falls on Shabbos?*

Yes,[178] except for the *esrog* -- after saying the *brochah, hanosein rei'ach tov bepeiros,* we may enjoy its lovely smell.[179]

---

177. *Mishnah Berurah* 596:3
178. *Rama* 658:2 Even a shofar which was formerly used for other purposes, will be *muktzeh* on Shabbos, since today we only use it for the mitzvah (*Shemiras Shabbos Kehilchasah* 28 Note 80).
179. *Rama* 658:2 During the rest of Sukkos, since there is a doubt whether to say a *brochah,* we avoid smelling the *esrog.*

Chapter Thirteen
Miscellaneous

1. *The earpiece has come off my glasses. Can I fix it?*

    On Shabbos, both the glasses and the earpiece are *muktzeh* because you might want to fix them, which is not allowed. On Yom Tov Chazal were lenient so that our *simchas* Yom Tov should not be diminished. They did not make the *gezeirah* that we might fix them and did not give the broken glasses the status of *muktzeh*.[180] Therefore you can use the glasses without the earpiece or even attach it in some ad hoc way e.g with a safety pin.[181]

2. *So if a leg falls off a chair which normally renders the chair muktzeh on Shabbos, it won't be muktzeh on Yom Tov?*

    Correct.

3. *Am I allowed to use frosting to write 'Happy Birthday' on my child's birthday cake if we are going to eat it?*

    No.[182] Because you are not truly writing those words for the

180. *Shulchan Aruch O.C.* 519:2
181. On Shabbos, there is a way of avoiding the *muktzeh* status by 'losing' the screw in an unusual way, e. g. causing it to be washed down the plughole of a sink, so that now the glasses can no longer be fixed, but need to be taken to an optician, and therefore the *gezeirah* does not apply. See *Do You Know Hilchos Shabbos?*
182. *Mishnah Berurah* 500:17 and *Shaar Hatziyun* 20

purpose of eating them, even though you might. It is rather to wish your child a happy birthday, and therefore not permitted.

4. *I have a bag of soup in the fridge and I am afraid that it will spill out. Can I tie a knot at the end of the bag so we will have soup for our seudah?*

If you couldn't have done it before Yom Tov, then it is allowed. However, if you have a better way of preventing the soup from spilling, like using a clip, that is preferable. On the same basis you would be allowed to sew up the skin of a chicken to keep stuffing inside.[183]

5. *We are not allowed to beat an egg on Shabbos because it looks as though we are planning to cook it.[184] It should be permitted on Yom Tov because we are allowed to cook. Is that right?*

Yes, there is no reason to forbid it.

6. *It's Seder night and I forgot to make the salt water. Can I do it now in the normal way?*

Assuming it's not Shabbos, yes.[185] On Shabbos you would just have to ensure that the ratio of salt to water is no more than two thirds.

7. *I forgot to take soup out of the freezer. Is it allowed to thaw in the pot where it will be ready to heat it up for the seudah?*

According to most opinions, yes.[186] If you want to follow all

183. *Shulchan Aruch* O.C. 509:3. See there the condition that the needle was already threaded before Yom Tov.
184. *Shabbos* 109a *Mishnah Berurah* 321:68
185. *Mishnah Berurah* 473:21
186. *Yom Tov Kehilchasah* 16:9 *Shemiras Shabbos Kehilchasah* 12 Note 31, *Shevus*

opinions, put some water in the pot first.

8. *Is it also better to put ice in water to thaw rather than in an empty pitcher?*

    Yes. Since it is easy to do it, you might as well fulfill all opinions.

9. *Oh no. Aunty Polly is visiting us this afternoon and I never toveled the cake knife she gave us for our last anniversary. Can I tovel it on Yom Tov?*

    Since you could have *toveled* it before Yom Tov you may not *tovel* it on Yom Tov. But if you have a co-operative non-Jewish neighbor, you can give it to him as a present, ask him if you can borrow it for today and then *tovel* it after Yom Tov.[187]

10. *I've just noticed that our oranges are from Israel. Can I ma'aser them on Yom Tov?*

    No, one is not allowed to *ma'aser* them on Shabbos or Yom Tov.[188]

11. *We are told to open bottles of drink and bags of food before Shabbos to avoid questions of Chillul Shabbos. Can we be more lenient on Yom Tov?*

    Since they could have been opened before Yom Tov, there is no leniency on Yom Tov.[189]

12. *Bubby has just come for tea on Yom Tov afternoon and brought my favorite bag of cookies. Can't I open the bag?*

Yitzchak Kellalei Yom Tov Section 12

187. Shulchan Aruch 323:7
188. *Ibid.* 524:1. The solution given in *Hilchos Eiruv Tavshilin*, to say the *nusach* with a condition – "If Yom Tov is today or tomorrow", does not apply to *Hafroshas Ma'aser*.
189. Like other *machshirei ochel nefesh*. See *Shulchan Aruch* O.C. 495:1

The best thing would be to open the bag in a way that it can't be used again and drop all the cookies into a plastic bag.

13.   *Our sukkah seems to be the most popular sukkah in the neighborhood, at least for flies. Can I spray them?*

Not to kill them.[190] But, as on Shabbos, you can spray into the air so that when they approach, they will be encouraged to fly elsewhere.

14.   *Are we allowed to boil an egg although the letters on the shell will be erased?*

Yes.[191]

15.   *Fido loves his meat freshly-cooked. I heard that there is a question whether we may cook for an animal on Yom Tov.*

There is a question in the Gemara, (*Beitzah* 21b) but the *halachah* is clear that one is not allowed to do any *melachah* for an animal on Yom Tov.[192]

16.   *But we won't have a moment's peace!*

If you're cooking for yourselves, you can put in some extra meat for your dog at the same time.[193]

---

190. There is a lot of discussion about this but most, if not all *Poskim*, do not allow killing a fly to avoid *tzaar* even though, in principle we may shecht an animal for eating. See *Yom Tov Kehilchasah, Miluim* 10.
191. Sefer Yom Tov *Kehilchasah* 6:18
192. *Shulchan Aruch* O.C. 512:3
193. *Rama Ibid.*

Chapter Fourteen
Death and Funerals on Yom Tov

1. *I'm only the guest rabbi for Yom Tov and one of the congregants has just been niftar on the first day of Yom Tov. What do I do?*

    If there is a danger that people will transgress the halachos of Yom Tov by telephoning relatives or travelling by car, there is no question that the funeral will have to be delayed until after Yom Tov. This is the halachah even if the delay will be a few days because perhaps Shabbos occurs straight after Yom Tov or there will be non-Jewish holidays when it is not possible to arrange a funeral.[194]

2. *Boruch Hashem this kehilah and all the family of the niftar are shomrei Shabbos so there is no danger of unauthorized chillul Yom Tov. So should we go ahead with funeral arrangements, then?*

    If you look up in your *Shulchan Aruch*[195] you will find that according to the strict *halachah*, a funeral may be arranged on the first day Yom Tov if non-Jews do all the *malachos* of the Torah which are required. This would include preparing *tachrichim* and digging a grave. Jews could dress the *meis* in the *tachrichim*, carry the coffin through the street to the

---

194. *Igros Moshe* O.C. 3:76
195. O.C. 526:1

hearse or to the cemetery and place the *meis* in the open grave. Non-Jews would have to fill the grave with earth after the burial. The *taharah* is not so simple because we have to avoid doing *melachos* during the washing process. In practice this means washing the *meis* by hand rather than with a cloth or sheet. If you arranged this, no-one could say you have done the wrong thing. If the cemetery is outside of the *techum* of the city, only those who are needed to do the burial itself are allowed to go, not others who are merely accompanying the *meis*.[196]

3.   *Is there an obligation to bury the deceased on the first day or is it permitted to delay the funeral so that Jews could participate in the funeral as normal?*

If it were clear-cut that this is how a funeral should be arranged on the first day of Yom Tov, we would be obliged to do so because there is a prohibition of delaying a funeral where it is not necessary. However there are those who hold that where the honor of the *meis* would not be compromised because, for instance, the *meis* could be kept in a refrigerated room, it is indeed better to wait until the second day of Yom Tov when Jews could participate much more fully and this would be more of an honor for the *meis*. There are also opinions which say that since non-Jews are involved anyway, it is better to let non-Jews do everything.[197] In practice, it is rare that a funeral is arranged for the first day Yom Tov.[198] However in Yerushalayim, where they are particularly careful not to leave a *meis* overnight, the *minhag* is to bury a *meis* on the first day of Yom Tov, using the services of non-Jews.

196. O.C. 526:6
197. *Mishnah Berurah* 526:12
198. See *Be'er Moshe* 2:45

4. *If a funeral will not take place, are we allowed to move the meis?*

A *meis* is *muktzeh* and may be moved only in order to maintain the *meis'* honor. In such a case we normally ask a non-Jew to take the *meis* by car to a refrigerated room until just before the funeral. This will maintain the honor of the *meis*.

5. *What about the second day of Yom Tov in Chutz La'aretz?*

Chazal were more lenient regarding the second day. Even if the person has just been *niftar* on the second day and if the funeral were not today it would be tomorrow, we are still allowed to do whatever is necessary, with a few exceptions. If there are non-Jews readily available, the *melachos* should be done by them[199] but if they are not, we may do the *melachos* ourselves. Certainly other aspects of the funeral which do not involve *melachos*, like carrying the *meis* and lowering the *meis* into the grave may be done by Jews even if non-Jews are available, as on the first day of Yom Tov. On the second day, Jews may fill up the grave, even making a mound on the top of the grave as is customary in a regular funeral.[200] For the *taharah*, we can use a clean sheet to put around the *meis* as we usually do but we are not allowed to squeeze or wring the sheet.[201]

6. *Is this also true for the second day of Rosh Hashanah?*

Yes. Unlike other leniencies of the second day of Yom Tov in *Chutz La'aretz* which do not apply on the second day of Rosh

---

199. The Sefardi *minhag* is for Jews to do the *melachos* even if non-Jews are available (*Shulchan Aruch* O.C. 526:4).
200. *Mishnah Berurah* 526:28. The *Shulchan Aruch HaRav* (526:9) holds that if there are non-Jews there, they should fill up the grave. Each place should do according to its custom.
201. *Rama* 526:4 and *Mishnah Berurah* 25-28

Hashanah, the leniencies concerning a burial *do* apply on the second day of Rosh Hashanah.[202]

7.   *If the cemetery is outside the techum, may the people go there to accompany the meis?*

Yes, on the second day it is permitted, in principle. However, except for the members of the *chevra kaddisha* who are required to actually perform the funeral, and are permitted to go by car if necessary[203], other people would have to walk. Even the immediate family, since they are not required to actually bury the *meis,* are not allowed to go by car even if it is driven by a non-Jew.[204] This is true even if there will be no *minyan* at the burial for *kaddish* to be said.[205] If a male mourner wants to substitute for one of the *chevra kaddisha* to take part in the actual burial, he may do so.[206] If there is nowhere for the members of the *chevra kaddisha* to stay until the end of Yom Tov, they are allowed to return.[207] If they cannot stay at the cemetery but there is somewhere they could stay without coming all the way back, they should stay there until after Yom Tov.[208]

---

202. *Shulchan Aruch* ibid
203. Only if it is very difficult for them to get to the cemetery by foot are they permitted (*Biur Halacha* 526:7). The *Mishnah Berurah* says that even those who are required, are only allowed to travel by horse *outside* the city. However the custom is that the *chevra kaddisha* may go by car, driven by a non-Jewish driver, even inside the *techum* (Rav Hillel Asher). If possible the car used should be a regular car so as not to bring attention to the fact the Jewish people are travelling on Yom Tov (*Nitei Gavriel Hilchos Yom Tov*).
204. *Gesher Hachaim* 17:2.4
205. *Ibid.*
206. *Be'er Moshe* 2:45-47
207. *Shulchan Aruch* 526:6. *Mishnah Berurah* 35.
208. *Mishnah Berurah* ibid, *Be'er Moshe* ibid.

8.   *If the niftar had asked to be buried elsewhere, even though there is a local cemetery, can we take him there on Yom Tov?*

No.[209]

9.   *Is it permitted to delay the funeral until the next day to allow relatives from another town to attend?*

Although there are opinions who do not allow this, Rav Elyashiv is reported to have allowed it.[210]

10. *When a funeral does take place on Yom Tov, do the mourners do kriah?*

No.[211] But they should do the *kriah* in the evening after Yom Tov.

---

209. *Mishnah Berurah* 526:22. *Yom Tov Kehilchasah* 24 Note 88 brings in the name of Reb Yisroel Yaakov Fisher that in a case that the *meis* has asked to be buried in Eretz Yisroel and by taking the *aron* to the airport on Yom Tov, the *meis* will be buried on what is the second day of Yom Tov in *Chutz La'aretz* but will be *Chol Hamoed* or *Isru Chag* in Eretz Yisroel, it is permitted to do so.
210. *Yom Tov Kehilchasah* 24 Note 69
211. *Shulchan Aruch* 526:11

Chapter Fifteen
Eiruv Tavshilin

1. *I'm a bit ashamed to admit that I have been making my eiruv tavshilin for years and I don't even know what the words mean. Can you help me?*

    Don't be ashamed. It's called living and learning and we all have to do it. The words *eiruv tavshilin* literally mean a mixture of cooked foods. This refers to the mixing together of foods cooked before Yom Tov and cooked on Yom Tov which is on *erev Shabbos,* to give us our Shabbos meal that week.

2. *Why do we have to do it?*

    In simple *halachic* terms, *Chazal* have told us to make an *eiruv tavshilin* before a Yom Tov which falls on *Erev Shabbos* to allow us to cook on Yom Tov for the next day which is Shabbos. Normally we are not allowed to cook on Yom Tov for after Yom Tov, even from the first day Yom Tov to the second day. On Shabbos we will not be allowed to cook because of the *halachos* of Shabbos but *Chazal* have said that if we make our *eiruv tavshilin* we can prepare for Shabbos and eat cooked foods as normal.

3. *Is there any source in the Torah for making an eiruv tavshilin?*

Chazal (*Beitzah* 14b) bring a hint from the Torah in that the *pasuk* says "Remember the Shabbos day to sanctify it." (*Shemos* 20:8). Why are we told to remember Shabbos? Could we ever forget Shabbos? Answer *Chazal*, "Yes. When Yom Tov is on Erev Shabbos we might be so involved in *Simchas Yom Tov* that we could forget about Shabbos and by the time we remembered, it might be too late to cook and we won't have anything to eat on Shabbos." By making an *eiruv tavshilin*, which requires us, as we shall soon see, to cook and bake before Yom Tov begins, we will always have at least something to eat on Shabbos.

4. *Did Chazal have any other reasons for this mitzvah?*

Yes. To remind us that as we may not even prepare on Yom Tov for Shabbos without making an *eiruv tavshilin*, certainly we are not allowed to do anything on Yom Tov for a weekday.[212]

5. *Does eiruv tavshilin allow me to do all melachos on Erev Shabbos for Shabbos?*

No. Only *melachos* to do with preparing food for the Shabbos meals.[213]

---

212. *Beitzah* 15b. The Maharal (*Netzach Yisroel* p.46) gives an explanation of *eiruv tavshilin* on the level of *remez*. He says that this world is like a weekday, the days of *Moshiach* are like Yom Tov and *Olam Haba* is like Shabbos. Someone who has begun preparing for *Olam Haba* in this world may continue during *Yemos Hamoshiach*. But someone who did not start preparing for *Olam Haba* in this world but only decides to start when the *nisyonos* of *Golus* will be over in *Yemos Hamoshiach*, will find that just as one may not cook on Yom Tov for Shabbos unless he started cooking before Yom Tov, also his efforts will count for naught. He is too late. This is the deeper meaning of *Yuma* 28b, which says that Avrohom Avinu kept the whole Torah, even *eiruv tavshilin*.

213. *Mishnah Berurah* 528:3 (*Yom Tov Kehilchaso* 25:20).

6. *What about rolling the sefer Torah to the place it needs to be for the Shabbos leining?*

Doing such a thing which is not a *melachah* and would be permitted for Yom Tov itself and the only question is whether it is not allowed because of preparing, the custom is to allow.[214]

7. *What is the ideal way to make eiruv tavshilin?*

On Thursday if Yom Tov begins on Erev Shabbos, or on Wednesday if Yom Tov falls on Thursday and Friday, take an important item of food like a piece of meat or chicken and cook (or roast) it for the *eiruv tavshilin* which is in effect cooking for Shabbos. Likewise bake some dough to make a complete *challah* which will be for the *eiruv tavshilin* and for Shabbos.

8. *Is it not good enough just to take a piece of meat which I have already cooked and some bread which I have already baked and use that?*

It is acceptable but not ideal.[215] Even if you didn't cook or bake but it was cooked or baked by a shopkeeper or food manufacturer it is still acceptable, just not the ideal.

9. *We always used an egg as the cooked food. Is this not acceptable?*

It is acceptable to use any cooked food, even *bedieved*, scrapings from the side of the pot! But it is a *hiddur mitzvah* to use important items of food.[216] If we remember that one

214. *Piskei Teshuvos* 528:3
215. *Biur Halacha* 527:6 s.v. *adashim*. A piece of cake is also accepted, *bedieved*, instead of bread (*Shevet Halevi* 8:129.2).
216. *Mishnah Berurah* 527:8 The *Aruch Hashulchan* 527:13 writes that a hardboiled egg is preferable to meat because it keeps better. This was in his

of the reasons for making *eiruv tavshilin* is to make sure that we have food for Shabbos as we mentioned above, it makes sense to use food which we usually eat in honor of Shabbos, i.e. meat and not just an egg.

10.   *What is the minimum amount of food we need to use?*

An egg size or at least an olive size.[217]

11.   *Right. I have the cooked food and the bread or matzah; what do I do now?*

Normally we hold the food and say the *brochah* "... *al mitzvos eiruv*". Then we say the following words. *Behadin eiruva yehei shara lon la'fuyei velivshulei velatmunei ulehadlukei shraga uleme'evad kol tzorchono miYom Tov l'Shabbos.* This means that with this *eiruv* it will be permitted [218] to bake, cook, wrap food (to keep it hot), light candles or oil lights and to do all our needs from Yom Tov to Shabbos. We can say this *nusach* in the original Aramaic but, if we don't understand the meaning of the words, we have to say the declaration in a language that we do understand.[219]

12.   *Is there any specific time to do the eiruv tavshilin on Erev Yom Tov?*

It should be done any time during the day of Erev Yom Tov until Yom Tov begins in the evening.[220] Obviously it's not a

---

days before fridges. This could well be the source of the common custom to use a hardboiled egg for *eiruv tavshilin*.
217. *Rama* 527:3
218. *Mishnah Berurah* 527:63
219. *Shulchan Aruch* and *Rama* 527:12 and Mishnah Berurah 40
220. *Mishnah Berurah* 44. See *Mishnah Berurah* 527:4: if one has brought in Yom Tov early by davening *Maariv* with a *tzibbur* before *shekia*, it is also too late

good idea to leave it until the last moment, because we can forget and it will be too late. Some people put up some kind of sign in the kitchen as a reminder to make *eiruv tavshilin* to avoid the risk of forgetting.

13. *What happens if someone accidentally eats the food of the eiruv tavshilin before we've done all our cooking on erev Shabbos?*

As long as there is an olive size of the *eiruv tavshilin* left, you can rely on it to cook on Erev Shabbos for Shabbos.

14. *Is it enough for one person to do the eiruv or must everybody do it?*

The head of the household can do it for the whole household.[221] He can appoint his wife or child over the age of bar/bas-mitzvah to do it on his behalf. Concerning guests who are eating their meals with their host and want to help with preparing the meal, the general custom is that they are also included. Some hold that guests and married children, especially if they are sleeping elsewhere, should make their own *eiruv*. Therefore, if they want to be *mehader,* they can ask the host to include them in the *eiruv* by asking a non-family member to lift up the food of the *eiruv* on their behalf when he makes the *eiruv* or they could make their own *eiruv* without a *brochah.*[222]

15. *What if I forget to make the eiruv tavshilin?*

It is a mitzvah for the *rav* of a *kehillah* to make an *eiruv tavshilin*

---

for *eiruv tavshilin* although, if one's wife has not brought in Yom Tov yet, some *Poskim* might allow her to make it still.
221. *Mishnah Berurah* 56
222. *Piskei Teshuvos* 17

for his *kehilah* in case anybody forgot or was unable to make their own *eiruv*. If you forgot, you could rely on the rav's *eiruv* to allow you to cook *etc.* on Yom Tov for Shabbos. When the rav makes *eiruv tavshilin* he has to ask an independent person[223] to lift up the food on behalf of all of his *kehillah* and then he takes the food back, says the same *nusach* but he adds on at the end, "....for all who live in this town".[224]

16. *So why does everybody make their own eiruv tavshilin? Let everyone just rely on the rav's eiruv!*

Clearly *Chazal* wanted us all to make an *eiruv* for the reasons we mentioned above. However according to the strict *halachah* one can appoint someone, including the rav to make the *eiruv* on his behalf.[225] If, however, you normally make your own *eiruv tavshilin* and therefore you have not appointed the rav to do it on your behalf and you forgot, this is the *halachah*. The first time, you can rely on the rav's *eiruv*. The second successive time you forget, however, you may not rely on the rav's *eiruv* and you will not have an *eiruv tavshilin*.[226]

17. *If I completely forgot for the second successive time but I remembered during Yom Tov, what can I do?*

If you were supposed to do the *eiruv tavshilin* on Wednesday because you are in *Chutz La'aretz* and the first or last two

223. A married son, even if he is financially dependent on his father, is considered an independent person (*Rama* 366:10).
224. *Rabbonim* in the major hospitals in Eretz Yisroel include in their communal *eiruv tavshilin* even patients who will come from another town for emergency treatment.
225. *Ibid.* 527:25.
226. *Ibid.* I said successive because only then can he no longer rely on the *rov's eiruv*. If he forgot but then the next time remembered and after that forgot again he could rely on the *rov's eiruv* again. *Kaf Hachaim* 48.

days of Pesach or Succos or the two days of Shavuos fall on the Thursday and Friday but you forgot until Yom Tov came in, there is a *halachic* solution —if you remembered during the first day. Since according to the Torah, Yom Tov is only one day but we are not sure whether it should be Thursday or Friday, you can take the food as normal and say the following, without a *brochah*[227]: "If today is really Yom Tov and tomorrow isn't, I don't need an *eiruv tavshilin*. If tomorrow is really Yom Tov and today is *Erev* Yom Tov, with this *eiruv* I will be allowed to bake and cook etc." as you should have done the day before. You can't do this on the first of the two days of Rosh Hashanah.[228]

18. *What can I do on Rosh Hashanah or if I only remembered on Erev Shabbos?*

If you have very helpful family or friends who did make an *eiruv tavshilin* and are willing to cook for you, you can make them the *halachic* owner(s) of your food by them taking the food into their home or by lifting the food up,[229] and they can cook for your Shabbos.[230]

19. *And if no-one so helpful is available?*

If there is no-one who can do this for you, you can take advantage of a leniency which *Chazal* gave for someone in your difficult situation and that is to bake one loaf, cook one dish and light one Shabbos light. If you don't like these options, tough! Don't forget another time!

227. *Mishnah Berurah* 527:74
228. *Shulchan Aruch* 527:22
229. But not by *kinyan sudar* (*Mishnah Berurah* 527:60)
230. *Shulchan Aruch* 527:20

20. *Assuming I have made the eiruv correctly, can I continue preparing throughout Erev Shabbos?*

You should finish all the cooking on Erev Shabbos some time before sunset, when Shabbos comes in, so that if a guest suddenly appeared you could offer him/her some of the food you have cooked. For this reason it is the custom in many places to start the Shabbos services, when Yom Tov falls on Erev Shabbos, earlier than normal to encourage people to finish their Shabbos preparations earlier. If there is an important need you can carry on cooking until just before sunset.[231] On the second day of Yom Tov we can be lenient with any need.[232]

Have a great Yom Tov and a great Shabbos

---

231. *Biur Halachah* 527:1 s.v *Al yedei eiruv.*
232. Ibid

Index